THE POLARITY HEALING
HANDBOOK

THE
POLARITY HEALING HANDBOOK

A Practical Introduction
to the Healing Therapy of Energy Balancing

Wilfried Teschler

Gateway Books, Bath
and Interbook Inc, San Leandro, Calif.

First published in English in 1986 by
GATEWAY BOOKS
19 Circus Place,
Bath, BA1 2PW

in the U.S.A. by
INTERBOOK Inc,
14895 E.14th Street,
San Leandro, CA 94577

First German publication 1984
as *Das Polarity Handbuch*
by Schangrila of Haldenwang

Translated by Pat Campbell

British Library Cataloguing in Publication Data:
Teschler, Wilfried
   The Polarity healing handbook.
   1. Therapeutic systems
   I. Title II. Das Polarity Handbuch.
English
   615.8   R733

ISBN 0-946551-18-9

Set in Century Schoolbook,
10pt on 11, by Wordsmiths of Street,
printed and bound in Great Britain
by WBC Print of Bristol and Ware of Clevedon.
Cover design by Studio B of Bristol.

Contents

Foreword

I have written this book for two reasons: First, to provide myself with a clear and systematic summary of polarity balancing and secondly because I considered it high time that this form of energy balancing work should be made available to more people than at present.

During the past few years I have used polarity balancing in groups and private sessions, gaining much practical experience of the value of different techniques. As time passed, it became quite clear that polarity balancing offered everyone the possibility of greater harmony within themselves, of being better grounded and more effective in all areas of their lives. I have extended the energy work familiar to healers by using meditative techniques, exercises to promote increased awareness and the generation of energy through massage. Finally, I have tried to present a psychological understanding of the basis of energy work.

It is my hope that polarity balancing will give as many people as possible the chance to escape from the dilemma of duality, the either/orness by which we are imprisoned in our egos, into the freedom of a balanced wholeness, a detached stillness through which we can rediscover our origins and make a connection to our life's purpose, enabling us to live our lives more fully.

Munchengladbach 1983

Wilfried Teschler

1. What are Polarities?

For some years now I have been using and developing polarity balancing techniques which have been known for some time in Germany and which have given me and others much pleasure and benefit.

The effect of polarity balancing is far-reaching, but time and time again I have been surprised by how energy contact between two people is so simple, yet how varied is the scope of polarity balancing. Many exercises and traditional points of energy contact are described, but I have added some of my own. Incidentally, I would welcome any other ideas from readers of how to extend the variety of contact, as well as any criticisms or suggestions about the book. We are all capable of 'lending a hand' in helping our partners and fellow beings to attain perfect balance, discover themselves and the peace of the 'zero point', where creative energy can be released. We find polarities in all our experience of life. The dark cannot exist without the light, inner feeling without the outer world. Nothing dies without having experienced life. Our own lives contain everyday examples of how we cannot have joy without sadness, or beauty without ugliness. A polarity system is concered with balancing complementary opposites. The point of balance is neither one nor the other polarity, and is like a third and new situation which has a reality and wholeness of its own. It is both at rest and in constant motion: we call it the zero point.

Polarity is found everywhere. Darkness cannot exist without light, the inner without the outer. Nothing can die without having grown. These are everyday natural processes which form part and parcel of our very existence.

Simply take a look at the polarity, the dichotomy of your live, calmly and objectively.

Polarities mould our lives. Many people are pulled to and fro between these polarities, others refuse to acknowledge their existence, whilst other flow with them, allowing themselves to be carried along by them; they *are* the polarity, one with the supreme wholeness.

We either live in and with this polarity and are thereby in harmony with it, or we simply block it and find ourselves in conflict. By so doing we are blocking the life force in and around us. Were I for instance to go about in winter dressed in light summer clothes, not accepting winter as the polarity of summer, it would come as no surprise if I were to catch a cold. The consequences of stubbornness (a blocking of energy) results in an illness.

Blockages such as discontentment, muscular tension, dis-ease, demonstrate, if we heed life's circumstances, how we have created an imbalance, how we have lost our unity. Nature's law of polarities demands that we should be constantly aware, weigh and harmonise ourselves with our environment. If we do not find this harmony, our very lives and our experience is inhibited, if not absolutely extinguished.

Polarisation in our Everyday Lives

We are all acquainted with exchanges of energy. A parent may pick up his or her child. If both child and parent are inwardly in harmony they will fuse into one unit. Sick children often seek the physical proximity of their mothers. They acutely sense the healing effect of an exchange of energy.

While it easy to distinguish joy from sadness in yourself or in another, to be aware of another's energy requires both sensitivity and practice. Usually if we shake hands with some one, all we notice is that this hand is warm or cold, damp or dry, firm or floppy. You should now begin to practice noticing his energy as well. If his hand is overcharged, you might notice a crackling when you shake his hand. If we shake hands with another with sensitivity, we also become more aware of him or her as a real person. Above all, this requires attention and feeling, not an analytical or judging mind, nor an over-expectant imagination. The reality is what you experience, and nothing else.

Energy exchange on a much deeper level occurs in sexual intercourse. A man and a woman who are appropriately matched carry opposite charges. If both allow their energies to flow during the sexual act, they arrive at the zero point: they become one. But if one withholds his energy, then at best it becomes a mere physical exercise, or a meeting of skin and bone.

What is Polarity Balancing?

If we pay attention to the circumstances of our lives, we shall see that such things as discontenment, muscle tension and illness are all symptoms of loss of equilibrium. Polarities set their stamp upon our lives. Many let themselves be torn this way and that between extremes; others pretend the extremes do not exist. The way forward, while experiencing the swings, is not to become identified or captured by the extremes. Then it becomes possible to discover balance, the unity of the zero point.

It is through the point of balance that the life force flows. By becoming imprisoned in our joy or our sadness, wanting to hold on to it, we create a block to this life force. The answer is to go with the experience of the polarity, but also to release it. Through being constantly alert to our surroundings we can come to terms with ourselves. If, on the other hand, we constantly block this experience, how can we expect our lives to unfold and widen?

Hold your hands with the palms about one foot apart. Gradually bring them together and try to be aware of a warmth or tickling of energy as they come close. Let the stream of life flow to and fro between your hands. It is a question of allowing yourself to experience it, not of actively willing it. You will notice that the more deeply you breathe, the more strongly the stream will flow. In balancing, this flow of fine energy between your hands washes away irregularities in your partner's body: over- or under-charging is evened out. This flow between your hands is stronger than any blockage of energy. It always finds the shortest and quickest way to restore the balance.

Each cell in the body strives towards its own state of harmony and the energy between your hands assists this process. With experience, when you carry out energy balancing, the body's natural need for harmony and the energy between your hands are often able to come together. There is then no longer any difference between your partner's life force and your own. Opposites are cancelled out, and you are one.

Photo 1: The flow of energy between the hands.

The Flow of Energy

In you and around you there is a continual flow. The life force flows to and fro between extremes, up and down, forwards and backwards. In a healthy and balanced person there exists an equal exchange between positive and negative poles. This manifests in a feeling of wellbeing, of inward composure, and outwardly in love and acceptance of others.

Exercise: Recognising the energy flow

You and your partner stand facing each other in a relaxed posture. His or her field of energy has a definite structure. Try to feel it. Don't try to imagine what it looks like. Try, rather, to be aware where it is overcharged. These regions of the body appear more obvious than those parts that are relaxed. You may feel them as being out of proportion. Many men are overcharged in the upper parts of their bodies, while many women have more energy in their lower parts. Avoid analysing – just be open to what you can see.

The energy in your partner's body may be flowing strongly or weakly. It may be light or dark. Perhaps his total energy is too great. If he has too little, he will appear debilitated and burnt out. There are as many variations in this as there are people and parts of the body. If you **are** unable to recognise the pattern of energy at the first attempt, just go on practising. You can always snatch a few minutes in the bus or in the street to practice observing.

When you have recognised how your partner's energy is distributed, speak to him or her about it. It is important to exchange impressions, for you will learn much more quickly how the energy manifests, and it is important for your partner to have the personal feedback. After this exchange, repeat the exercise. It may well be that the energy field has now changed. Don't force yourself and your partner in this exercise, for that would result in a block being created between you.

A human being carries a positive charge in relation to the earth's energy. If the exchange of energy between the earth and someone is restricted or blocked, he or she will feel uprooted, forced, inexplicably restless. He has no place where he belongs and does not feel at home anywhere. In

12

Photo 2: a) From the front

b) From the side.

addition he does not have 'both feet on the ground'. For a person with such a block it is very difficult to adopt an appropriate attitude to something in his life, to maintain it and, if necessary, to relinquish it.

Exercise: Stand upright with the feet about a foot apart. Direct your attention *into* and *onto* your feet. Visualise in your mind's eye your feet forming roots connecting them with the earth. Let the roots grow and flourish. As they grow your development will expand with them. In time your roots will reach the centre of the earth and become anchored there.

If you are undercharged in relation to the earth's energy, then according the the law of equalisation Mother Earth will give you energy, and you will feel better. If you are overcharged, let the excess energy drain away into the earth. Do not force yourself either to give or to take, just let it happen. Between Mother Earth (–) and Father Sun (+) there exists a perpetual exchange of powerful quanta of energy which maintains all living things and maintains the Earth in her course. Someone who has established a good connection with the earth's field of force and has become unified with it will now have polarity with the sun. You should realise that you have now reached the stage of development with is the way of unity with the sun. Continual exchange with the sun brings you enormous vitality, creativity and creative power. If you block this you will quickly become crushed, depressed and exhausted. Once you have consciously made a good connection, you will always find your way back to the energy of the sun.

Exercise: Forming an energy channel
Stand as described in the previous exercise. Stretch your arms above your head. Visualise the sun's energy pouring in through your hands and through the top of your head. Open yourself completely. Let the energy flow right through you. If you are completly open, with practice, you will be connected by energy to the sun and to the earth. You will have become a channel and the stream of energy will purify you. But take care not to hold onto any energy. Static energy always has a bad effect.

As time goes on you will be led by this work into further polarities and will combine them in yourself. The final result will be to experience unity. When this stage is reached, polarities will cease to have any hold over you. Polarity balancing in this comprehensive form gives you the possibility of losing your blocks and of coming ever nearer to your own Self.

The unity of all poles is the zero point. It is everything, and it is nothing.

Yin and Yang

2. Working with Polarity

Clothing

During energy balancing work, you should always wear loose, comfortable clothing made from natural fibres, as these allow a better flow of natural physical energy. Man-made fibres like nylon obstruct the energy, and wearing them leads to its stagnation on the skin, which may result in a feeling of discomfort. Tight clothing also has a restricting effect. Bras, watches and girdles should not be worn while working. It is also difficult if you or your partner are feeling hungry or too full.

Outward Posture

Your outward posture has a considerable influence on your energy flow. If you tense up, you will cause serious energy blocks. Before starting work, centre your attention, and place it systematically on each part of the body, starting with the feet, moving up through the trunk to the arms and hands, giving particular attention to your shoulders, neck and face. Note any stress points and relax them. During massage, too, adopt an easy and relaxed posture.

The opposite of tension is slackness, an unconscious letting go. You are then half asleep, so energy flows slowly, too slowly for you to be able to work on polarity balancing. Wake up, be on the alert!

Inner Attitude

Life energy does not allow itself to be manipulated. It goes its own way and often this is not what you expect. Don't meddle with it. Let the life force take its own course. It is more intelligent than reason. If you go along with it, in the end you will always see that it has chosen the best way. Let yourself be guided by it. As time goes on you will become ever more receptive to how it responds to the connection between you and your partner, and with the flow of life.

Preparatory Exercise: Earthing
People who are well earthed cannot easily be upset. I have found them to be more efficient, better prepared for action and able to respond to circumstances. The essential prerequisite of all polarity work lies in being well earthed.

Whenever you have a spare moment and the inclination, stand upright and form a connection with the earth through your feet, as described in the last but one exercise. As time goes on it will give you ever greater firmness and stability.

Preparatory exercise: Hara breathing
Stand upright. Place your hands on your stomach just below the navel. This area is called the Hara. When breathing in, direct the breath towards this chakra or energy center. Then after five to ten respirations drop your hands. Next breathe in towards the Hara and then, as you exhale, visualise the energy going out through the legs into the earth. Do this ten to twenty times.

Repeat this exercise, but breathe out through the arms ten to twenty times.

Repeat again and breathe out through the arms and legs simultaneously – about five times. Try to be aware of your feelings of what has happened.

A further exercise is useful to purify the energy before polarity work.

Preparatory exercise; Releasing retained energy:
Stand upright and become aware of your whole body. Open yourself up and observe your body quietly and calmly. Let the superfluous energy around your body drain away into the earth. All you have to do is to let go of it; everything else happens of its own accord. Take time over this exercise. It may be helpful to rid yourself, first of all, of the excess energy around your body, and only then, the inner excess energy.

16

These last three suggested exercises are intended as preparation for polarity work, but the last exercise, for example, is suitable for ridding yourself of anger, headache, restlessness, lack of interest, tension, etc. It is also useful for putting you in touch with the special energy required by a change of circumstance.

My experience shows that it is enormously important to start polarity work in a state of harmony. Your movements will then be more assured and the energy will be able to flow well.

Photo 4: The Bow

Recognition of energy blocks

Not everyone is able to recognise the distribution of energy in his partner right from the start. Sometimes intensive practice is necessary. The following bio-energetic exercises, the Bow and the Elephant, are a good way to recognise under-charging or over-charging.

The Bow
Stand upright with your feet about a foot apart, your toes turned slightly inwards. Bend your knees a little and stretch your abdomen and your pelvis forward, so that your body forms a bow, with your shoulders and your heels in a straight line. Relax your head with your chin more or less parallel with the ground. Stretch your arms and hands up as far as possible. Make sure that the the soles of your feet are wholly on the ground.

Try out this posture first by yourself, so that you get the feeling of it. Then ask your partner to adopt it. Observe him/her carefully:
Are his hands clenched into fists or stretched up rigidly?
Are his arms crooked?
Is his head bent sideways?
Are his shoulders tense?
Is he breathing in a deep or a shallow way?
Is he standing crookedly?
Is his pelvis drawn in or crooked?
Are both feet absolutely flat on the floor?
Is his weight distributed evenly on his two legs?
Is the left half of his body different from the right?

17

These questions should form the basis of your observation. You will find that no two people do the Bow exercise in exactly the same way or feel the same about it.

Ask your partner how his/her body feels. Is she aware of all parts of her body or is she more aware of one part? Has she a good contact with the earth? Does she feel her forehead, her chest, her pelvis, her abdomen, her back, her legs, her feet, her toes? Go over all the parts of the body with your partner while she puts her attention on each part and tells you her feelings and observations. This observation training enhances consciousness of the body.

Shut your eyes and see if you can be aware of your partner's body. What do you know about him? In the picture which comes into your mind, has he got legs? What do they look like? Has he got arms? Is his chest large or small? Is the pelvic region sufficiently developed? How does the energy flow in his body? In your mind's eye do you see dark spots in or around his body? Is light energy invaded by dark energy? Can you recognise a continual flow of light energy in his body? Observe these phenomena without anticipating anything and see what effect they have on you.

The Elephant

After the Bow exercise, your partner should *slowly* and *consciously* go over into the Elephant posture. He gradually bends forward and downwards, rolling the spine, vertebra by vertebra, until his fingertips lightly touch the ground. His knees remain slightly bent. The coccyx (the 'tail' on the base if your spine) should be raised as high as possible until it sets up a slight vibration in the thighs and in the pelvis, and the heels should always be in contact with the ground.

During this exercise you can make additional observations. How does his back appear – too stiff or too slack? Does the movement take place towards the left or the right? Does he have difficulty with the position of his head? Do his knees remain slightly bent? How is his breathing? Is his neck strained? How are his abdominal muscles and his forehead?

Ask you partner how he feels before, during and after the exercise. What he tells you will give you further information about his whole state of energy and any special blocks in his body. After talking about it, it is helpful to repeat these exercises.

18

Not only do the Bow and Elephant exercises give an indication about blocks, but they also intensify the flow of the whole life energy. You should repeat both exercises, to help you recognise energy blocks.

Now you are probably able to form a better picture of the state of your partner's body energy.

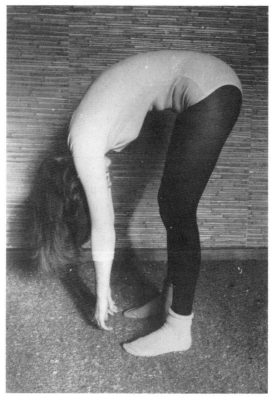

Photo 5: Elephant

Photo 6: Right hand just above the heel, left hand under the sole of the foot.

Polarisation of individual parts of the body

For ease of reference in the following description of the contacts used in energy balancing, I have begun with the lower part of the body and worked upwards.

It may be that in your partner's case it is the energy in the back which should be balanced first, then in the legs and then in the head. There are no hard and fast rules to be followed, but rather the procedure must be tailored to fit your partner's condition at any given moment. The best guide is the life force. It will show you how to carry out the right exercises in the right order. Every person and every situation is new and different. Adjust to this and allow yourself to be carried along with it. For example, if your partner is retaining unharmonised energy in his head, then you should of course begin with this part of his body. Through exercise comes experience. Through experience comes knowledge. After knowledge comes intuition. After intuition comes direct action.

Photo 7: Right hand just above the heel, left hand round the toes.

The Feet

Since very few people pay attention to their feet, you will find that there is often very little energy in this part of the body. That is why so many people often get 'cold feet'.

When the energy has been equalised, the foot chakras (the energy centres on the soles of the feet) can work more effectively. They regulate energy charging and discharging from the earth. In doing so, they regulate the charging of the chakras or energy centers in other parts of the body. A balanced flow of energy in the feet constitutes a basis for a feeling of well-being throughout the rest of the body.

The following pictures show how the foot energy can be harmonised.

Hold one foot, as shown in photo 6. Look at this foot, be conscious of it. Take in the structure of the foot: the bones, the ankle, the joints, the muscles, the veins and arteries, the skin. How does the foot feel to the touch? Is it firm and hard? Does it seem underused or overworked? Feel the temperature. How is it overall? Are there warm places in

Photo 8: Right hand just above the heel, left hand above the toes.

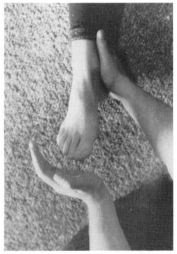

Photo 9: Left hand on the sole of the foot, right hand on the upper third of the calf.

the foot? Take in all these impressions.

Concentrate now on the energy picture. Be relaxed. Direct your attention *into* your partner's foot. Let the energy picture of the foot appear in inner vision. Where is there no energy? Where is it black or grey, where does it flicker? Is the energy fresh and flowing? Does it run across the foot? Make your observations without judging them.

Now direct your attention towards your hands and the flow of energy between them. Breathe quietly, taking calm, deep breaths. Open your arms and hands to the flow of the life force. Concentrate on your hands. Keep your eyes effortlessly shut. Follow the course of the life force with your inward eye. Look but do not judge. Observe whether the energy structure of the foot begins to be changed by the stream of life force and, if so, how. Be alert!

You should make these observations every time you make a new contact in balancing work. They will help you to work in accordance with polarity. In time the more subtle observations will arise of their own accord. Just go on practising.

During the polarity work, your partner will have various sensations. These may range from nothing to a slight twitching, through a feeling of wellbeing, to an absolute 'high'. Ask him about them. If the energy held in the foot is seriously blocked only a slight change will be felt, or none at all. If the energy is already mobile and light before being balanced, the change will quickly be seen by you and felt by your partner.

It is extremely difficult to make energy suddenly flow if its 'structure' has become 'hardened' over the years. It requires patience to free 'solidified structures'. Your partner must have time to experience the free flow of energy.

During the equalising process, it is important to keep taking rests of several minutes. The channels for the flowing energy open slowly and the retained energy must first flow down. Listen to your intuition, which will tell you when and for how long you should rest. You will know this provided you remain alert. Stop your activity before the life force ceases to flow to and fro between your hands.

Feet and calves

This polarity contact should establish the connection of energy between the foot and the rest of the body. A short distance above the heel, many people have an energy block, cutting off the supply to the foot. The left hand, as shown in photos 7 and 8, can change its position.

Photo 10: Left hand on the calf, right hand at the front of the thigh.

The Knee

Much stagnant energy is found in the region of the knees, which makes them psychically stagnant and sometimes even immovable physically. When you are balancing stagnant regions, take care that you always massage your partner downwards, towards the feet, then the energy released can flow downwards more easily.

When massaging the leg, begin roughly at the middle of the thigh and massage slowly downwards without pressure. If your hands feel thick after massage or if there is a tingling in them, it means that you have taken in part of the stagnant energy. Shake the energy out of your hands, as if you were shaking off drops of water. If that is not enough, hold your hands under cold running water and let the energy be washed away. You cannot expect to work well with someone else's energy in your hands. Besides, this dark energy will spread through your body and establish itself there.

After balancing sessions, check the air in the room in which you have been working. Often there is still so much released energy in the room that it is essential to air it.

The lower extremities have an energy connection with the rest of the body. An energy block is often found in the hip joints, so that the legs become 'cut off' from the trunk. The exercise 'swinging the hip when walking' produces a loosening of the energy in this region of the body.

The polarity contacts shown on photos 10 - 13 complement each other very well.

Photo 11: Left hand on the shinbone, right hand behind the thigh.

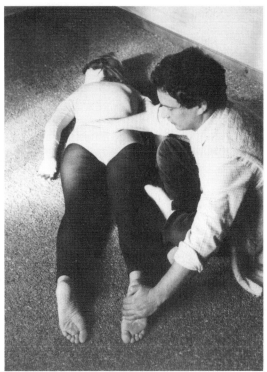 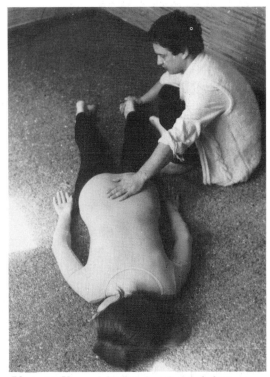

Photo 12: Your partner lying face downwards. Your left hand on her right foot, your right hand at the base of her spine on the pelvis.

Photo 13: Your right hand on her left foot, your left hand at the base of her spine on the pelvis.

The Leg Circuit

By means of this polarity contact the energy in both legs is harmonised simultaneously. The life force of the legs is united in the pelvis which facilitates coordination in walking. It stabilises both legs and strengthens the flow of energy between the pelvis and the legs. After polarity balancing of each leg separately, this contact can be used to harmonise the whole.

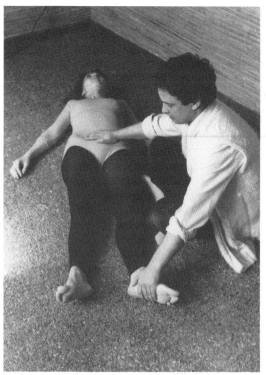 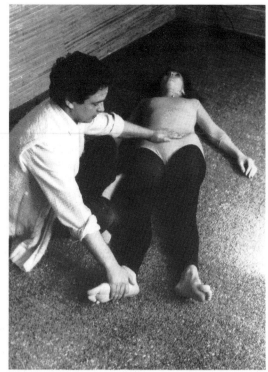

Photo 14: Right hand above the pubic bone, left hand holding your partner's left foot.

Photo 15: Left hand above the pubic bone, right hand holding your partner's right foot.

Photo 16: Partner lying on back, your right hand on her left heel. The heel is raised slightly. Your left hand on her right heel, also slightly raised.

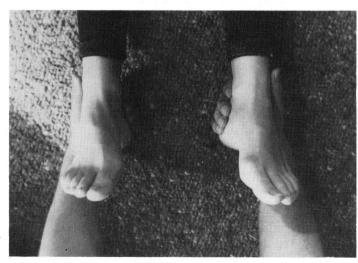

The Pelvis

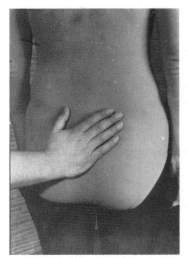

Photo 17: Right hand on the back wall of the pelvis.

The pelvis is the region where the energy of the earth rising from below through the legs meets and is united with the energy of the sun coming down from above. From the pelvis, this mixed energy spreads throughout the whole body. Male and female forces unite and through their union produce life. The pelvis is not only the pole or pivot biologically speaking, it is also the centre where our channels of energy cross. Besides this, in its lower, back part is situated the source of the life energy which flows up the back along the spinal column. Our vital force comes from the pelvis. It it cannot flow freely, then we cannot draw on our full potential for self-realisation. It is my impression that most people draw on only about 2% of their total force! Only a very few achieve higher vitality.

Free-flowing pelvic energy brings with it the fulfilment of sexuality. Polarity towards the other sex is completely developed. The whole of life becomes richer and more fulfilled.

Exercise: Hip-swinging sideways
First get into your usual stance. Observe how you hold your pelvis. Then let your pelvis swing ligtly to and fro, while remaining loose overall. Let the swinging become stronger. You will probably notice that it can swing out further on one side. An impeded swing points to a block. After the exercise lie down on the ground and sense your pelvis.

Exercise: Swinging the pelvis forwards and backwards
Stand upright and let your pelvis swing forwards and then backwards. Do not make use of the knees or the abdominal muscles! Move only your pelvis. Observe your feelings. After this exercise notice once again how it feels inside your pelvis.

Exercise: The union of energy from the earth and sun in your pelvis
Stand upright, legs and feet apart. Let the earth energy flow into your pelvis through these channels. Open your head and your trunk and let the sun energy stream into your pelvis. There the energies will be united. Let this

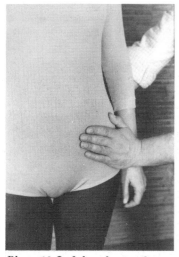

Photo 18: Left hand over the left pelvic cavity.

25

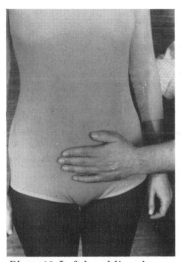

Photo 19: Left hand lies above the pubic bone.

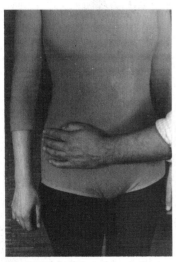

Photo 20: Left hand over the right pelvic cavity.

united force irradiate your whole body. This exercise creates greater harmony and directs attention towards the pelvis. The energies imprisoned there are slowly liberated and through performing this exercise we become more closely connected with the earth and sun, which give and maintain life. If it seems necessary, let the earth/sun energy flow down again away and out through your legs. Try to feel exactly what is good for your development.

I have mostly found this area to be dark with imprisoned energy. An excess of energy has been stowed away in the middle of the abdomen, which has resulted in very great fear, even mortal terror. The left side is the seat of energy which makes a person tearful and withdrawn; the right side houses energy which makes a person brutal and can even make him go berserk if it is released into daily life. These energies often feel as hard as granite, It usually takes a very long time before they are loosened and flow away.

If it is difficult, even impossible, at times to understand the situation by means of reason, use the polarity word meditation described on page 82 which promotes awareness of a different kind.

Working with polarity energy is no magic means of developing personality. A slow process of development must take place and, for this, inward cooperation is a necessary preliminary. It is impossible to make retained energy flow if your partner does not allow it to happen. To the casual observer it may seem that your partner's role is to be merely passively receptive but in reality s/he must adopt an active attitude towards change and give his/her consent to it.

I would like to mention this positive attitude towards change and further development particularly in connection with work on the pelvis, because it is here that blocks occur which many people find difficult to get rid of. If energy in the pelvis does not change for a long time, that is if it hardly flows, or does not flow at all, it may derive from your partner's lack of cooperation. Speak to her about it. See too, when working on the pelvis, that your partner is well earthed. If she has a bad connection with the earth, the retained energy, even if partly freed, will be largely unable to flow away.

The following photo (21) shows how the flow of energy between pelvis and feet is established and increased.

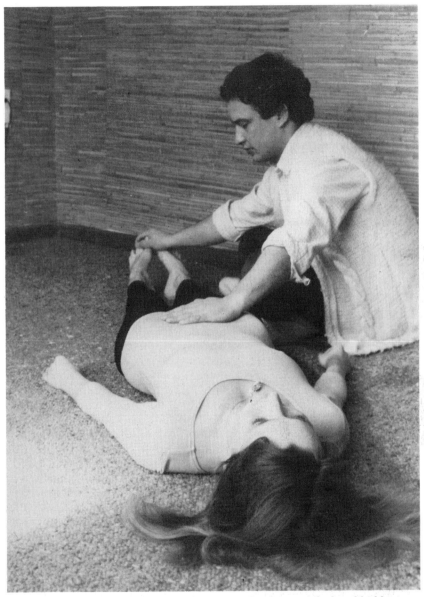

Photo 21: Left hand on the pelvis above the pubic bone, right hand holds the toes of both feet.

Photo 22: Right hand from the outside on the right pelvic cavity, left hand on the inside of the right thigh.

Photo 23: Left hand from the outside on the left pelvic cavity, right hand on the inside of the left thigh.

Because the legs can be opened, it is easier for the energy to drain away.

Exercise: Connecting the thigh with the pelvis.
Your partner lies on his back. You are beside him on the left, and you put your left hand on his right thigh. You put your right hand over his left pelvic cavity. Then you go round his feet and put your right hand on his left thigh and your left hand over his right pelvic cavity.

In this contact, as in all others, pay attention to the flow of energy which is released. Remain alert, recognise when it is appropriate to take a rest, or when balancing through this contact must be stopped. It will sometimes happen that the same contact will have to be made for different lengths of time on the two sides of the body. Look out for this.

By means of these polarity contacts the retained energy at the top of the legs and in the region of the genitals can be loosened and released. A circle of retained energy is often found around the genitals, by which they are cut off from the energy of the body and full sexual feeling is thereby inhibited. The flow of energy which is then set in motion runs down the inner side of the legs to the feet and from there it streams out. In this way a further channel has been opened down which the 'solid' energy in the pelvis can flow and the tension in the legs is relieved. Another possibility of directing the life force through the lower pelvic region is as follows:

Place your left hand on your partner's pelvis, just above the pubic bone. Your right hand is laid on the inner side of each thigh alternately.

In many people the energy of the pelvis is isolated from that of the trunk. In such a case there is a girdle or plane of energy in the upper region of the pelvis at about the height of the waist. The sexual energy present in the pelvis does not penetrate into the consciousness and since it is either restricted or entirely unnoticed it is not available – and therefore, of course, presents no conscious threat. We must realise that our culture is hostile to sexuality. This gives rise to a situation in which the sexual energy of the pelvis is killed off or held in check.

The whole body in the region of the waist is here divided above and below into active and passive forces. People who have to assert themselves all their lives, or who think

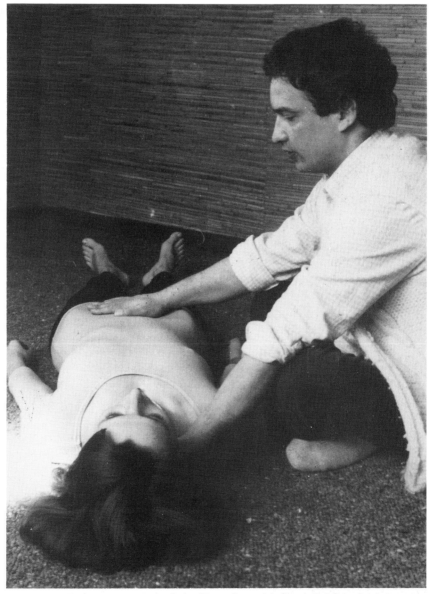

Photo 24: Right hand on the pelvis above the pubic bone, left hand on the nape of the neck.

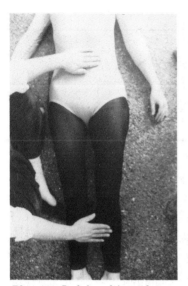

Photo 25: Left hand just above the navel, right hand on the middle of the shin.

that they should do so, have an exaggeratedly pronounced upper part of the body. Such people are more extrovert and feel well when they are being active. But seen as a whole, they are lacking in a certain passivity, in an ability to let themselves go. They come off badly as far as enjoyment is concerned. Men especially have a tendency in this direction.

If the region below the waist is strongly emphasised, then such a person is more likely to have a pronounced tendency to passivity. He will be more stable and will for this reason often appear rigid. He will like to retreat into domestic cosiness and is more introvert.

These one-sided divisions of energy set their mark on the body picture and on the whole way of living, acting and thinking. The main tendency of education is also reflected in the present over-emphasis on either this upper or the lower half of the body. People are educated either for an active or a passive life.

If the energy of a person's body at the waist is extended upwards or downwards and distributed better, then he will feel and enrichment of his life. Someone who is primarily active will achieve more calmness and composure; a passive person will become more decisive and take pleasure in action. Better distribution of energy downwards is shown on photo 25.

A possible way of freeing the imprisoned energy below the waist and directing it upwards is a follows: you place your right hand on the pelvis above the pubic bone and your left hand on the nape of the neck (photo 24). As a variation of this contact, you can place your left hand on the upper part of your partner's chest. Find out which variation is suitable for your partner and yourself. It may be that the energy will flow better if you hold your thumb over the navel. This polarisation brings more harmony to the lower parts of the body.

You can achieve greater harmony in the upper region with the following polarisation (photo 26).

These two polarity points are especially suitable for achieving a gradual improvement in the distribution of body energy upwards and downwards. The block at the waist first becomes softer and with increasing conscious-

30

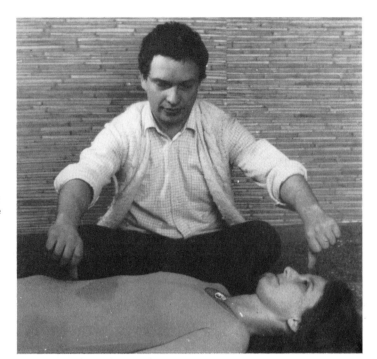

Photo 26: Hold your right thumb over the navel, your left thumb over the root of the nose

ness dissolves altogether.

Work on body energy in the pelvis and the distribution of energy upwards and downwards establishes three facts:

1. A special structure of energy results in a specific mode of life and action.

2. Every change in the structure of body energy in any one region results in structural changes in other regions.

3. Development follows a certain process.

Each human being exhibits his own particular distribution of retained and flowing vital energy. This distribution which is peculiar to him enables him to see himself and his surroundings in a certain way. The ground plan of this distribution of energy was laid down and became established during the early years of his life.

All these energy structures keep a person in his own special groove. For this reason many people think that this groove is their true way of life and it is their duty to remain in it, instead of adopting a way that would bring them happiness – namely to *be* inside themselves and to let themselves be carried along by the tide of life.

31

Every release of 'rigid' energy, especially in the pelvis, leads to further liberation. This affects the whole energy structure of the body. For example, if the pelvis is freed, that in turn leads to a change in the energy of the legs. That person will then have a better connection with the earth. This in turn leads to greater self-confidence and therefore greater scope for action. Greater scope for action probably gives a person a better perspective from which she can joyfully set about exploring the world and herself. She will use her arms and her head more; she will be more vital, feel and experience more; and this, too, will lead to further changes in physical energy.

The growth of development is a sometimes wavy, but always rising curve:

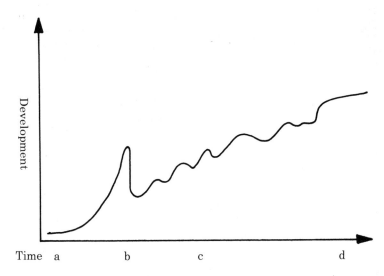

First of all the seeker finds out about methods and possibilities of development (a). Then usually a markedly euphoric upward trend sets in (b), ending in disillusion. During the euphoric phase, the illusion often exists that developmental work must always bring a feeling of well-being. Disillusion results in coming to terms with outward reality. It takes a person some time to get over this often harsh disappointment. The course of the development which follows is marked by more or less strong ups and downs, having, however, an upward tendency (composure and vitality).

32

At some point in his development a person finds himself, and develops further without any great variations (d). This is when he has had the first positive experience of his self-development.

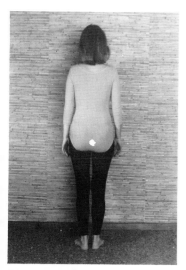

Photo 27: Back view: energy point at the coccyx.

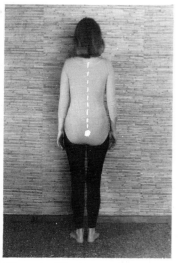

Photo 28: Weakened life force.

The Back

Unblocked life force in the back runs up the spine between the coccyx and the head. Its course can be interrupted in several ways. The energy may be too weak or unevenly distributed or it may be flowing in the wrong channel. There is a clear relationship between the strength and course of the energy in the back and the whole manner in which a person behaves. With some people their vital energy becomes stuck at a single point in the region of the coccyx. They do not like themselves and are not open towards themselves. Very often they seek to compensate for their lack of self-esteem by taking part in social activities. This attempt is usually only wishful thinking and cannot be realised, because they do not have the strength. Such a distribution of energy is a sign that the people who have it are in need of help, but help is something such people find difficult to accept.

Life force and individuality have shrunk to a single point.
The more freely the vital energy streams upwards through the back to the head, the more active a person will be. He has more 'backbone'. However, weakened or interrupted life force is more frequently found.

You can detect the weakened flow mostly in the lower part of the back, and non-specific pains in the spine are symptoms reported from time to time. People with these problems can stand upright only with difficulty. Often, too, you can detect the weakened flow of energy between the shoulder blades. Here it is a sign of difficulty in action – in giving and receiving. Interruptions in the flow of the life force occur in most people in the same places. This induces the feeling that their 'back is broken'. Life seems no longer bearable. The interruptions are often accompanied by a band of energy right round the body. It may be pelvic, abdominal, chest, shoulder and nape of the neck, a forehead band or it may be sited at the top of the head.

People whose energy drains away forwards feel depressed. Their life force presses downwards. The social circumstances of the moment usually play a great part in this, nevertheless there is a good chance of restoring the life force in a relatively short time, and hence of regaining vitality. Then the feeling of being at the mercy of outward circumstances will also disappear. The person concerned will have more power to intervene actively in the circumstances which are weighing him down and to alter them in his own favour.

Life energy can also go off course. People in whom energy flows off to the right behave and feel in a more masculine and active way. Energy flowing off to the left produces a more feminine and passive attitude. A man experiencing the first mode, and a woman the second would probably each experience a sense of well-being in their own sex.

Men with an energy flow which runs off to the right usually appear exaggeratedly masculine, but this blown-up image gives an unconvincing impression, suggesting unreliability. If the energy flow in men is off to the left, then they appear passive and feminine, attaching great importance to externals. This can go to such extremes that they appear with hair curled like a woman, use makeup and are artificially refined in their movements. Whatever their age they have very little masculinity about them.

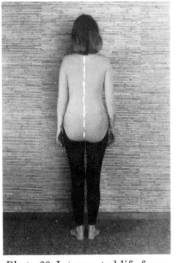

Photo 29: Interrupted life force.

Photo 30: Side view – energy draining away forwards.

Women with energy flowing off to the right are strongly masculine. To others they often appear crude and determinedly active. Many women whose life energy takes this course are found in political groups or are career women. Women whose energy flows off course to the left are very feminine and delicate and are often small in stature. They are very close to the child-woman type, are extrememly passive and give a loveable impression.

This categorisation of the way energy flows in different types of people can of course furnish only the crudest points of reference as a basis for your own observation. The way an individual feels and the way he presents himself depends largely on the whole distribution pattern of free-flowing and stagnant energy.

A further basic variation of the flow of energy in the back is branching.

Such people usually possess a strong backbone, but they feel torn apart. This distribution of energy can be seen in many schizophrenics, but of course this does not mean that everybody with such an energy picture is a schizophrenic. If you suspect that your partner is suffering from some psychological disorder, refer him to a specialist whom he can trust.

The more obviously the life energy in the back is branched, the greater will be difficulties experienced by the person in question. He is always torn between at least

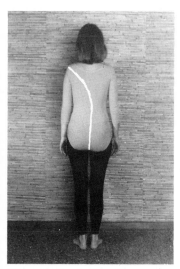

Photo 31: Back view. Energy flowing away to the left.

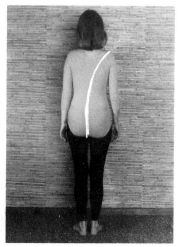

Photo 32: Back view. Energy flowing away to the right.

two extremes. Either his is much too impulsive in his actions, or else he lapses into lethargy. Such extremes make life difficult for his associates.

Another energy structure which often arises is branching off in the region of the shoulders (photo 34). People of this type always have a lot to bear, and if you question them closely about it, you will find that they mostly want to bear it. However, in spite of their burden, which is usually of an external nature, they give an impression of stability and dependability. Nothing is too much trouble for them. It is true that they sometimes groan under their burden, but they do not shake it off. If your partner comes with such a distribution of energy, speak to him about it; ask him about his burden. See if he can connect his outward life situation to the inward distribution of his life energy. Perhaps he will change his social conditions or his attitude towards them. Both things must work together if a lasting stabilisation of his life energy in its normal course is to be achieved.

Although people with this branching off of energy in the shoulder region can get on well with their difficulties, their lifestyle is usually anything but satisfactory, and does not correspond to their actual possibilities. A compensating, stabilising and strengthening energy structure is shown in photo 35.

Photo 33: Back view.
Branching out of energy.

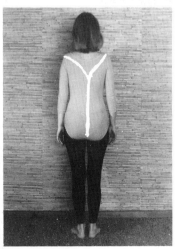

Photo 34: Back view. Energy branching off in the region of the shoulders.

36

The life energy in the backbone runs continually and is not interrupted. To left and right, running through the back, two channels of retained energy have appeared. They act as stabilisers for the relatively weak life energy in the middle. These stabilisers draw their power from the life energy in the middle of the back. That means that the apparent stabilisation must be removed if the stream of life energy is to flow again in its original strength.

People with this distribution of energy have often in the course of their lives had the feeling that they were not strong enough to master their existence and have therefore built up an artificial resistance. Now that that tiring period of their lives lies behind them, they give the impression of being excessively disciplined and are scarcely able to see what lies to right and to left of them. They go through life with blinkers on, so to speak. They are very security-conscious and like to avoid situation which set their life in motion, since all movement is seen as disorder. When once they have decided on a new direction, they pursue it with the same perseverance and relative rigidity as before. This kind of energy pattern gives a person the feeling of being correct, serious, dependable and straightforward.

Another energy pattern, which often occurs, appears as follows:

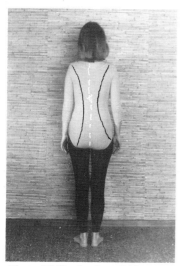

Photo 35: Back view. Life energy weakened in the middle.

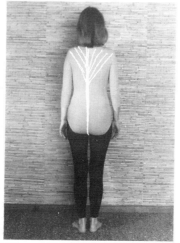

Photo 36: Back view – released energy distributed in the shoulders.

37

People with this energy pattern appear dogmatic and aggressive; apparently one can only submit to them or avoid them. They themselves mostly feel left alone and sometimes lonely. To them other people often appear as a threat to their independence. In their youth they have mostly had to stand up to a mother or father who was supposedly or actually over-powerful.

These descriptions are points of reference for your own observations. I have described the distribution of energy in the back as I have often observed it. I recognise that it is most clearly reflected in the world of feeling and experience.

Strangely enough, life energy which is not in its right channel has more effect on the whole of life than retained energy in one whole section of the body. To put it basically: wrongly directed life energy means that a person finds himself in a wrong way of life. He is in a cul-de-sac from which he can probably never escape without outside help. It is very important to speak about these matters with our patients and our partners in individual sessions and in groups, since an overall picture of the relationship between many things can first be established by means of reason and this forms a stable basis for all further development. Through such an understanding the readiness for change – in the direction of zero point – is increased and more inner and outer flexibility is achieved.

Photo 37: Right hand on the coccyx, left hand at the base of the neck.

Photo 37 shows the polarity contact which intensifies the flow of energy in the spine. This contact is useful when the flow of life energy in this channel is so weakened that your partner feels scarcely any change in his back or no appreciable change at all. Trust your inner eye to take in the course and change in the flow of life energy. If it is visible at only one point, at the coccyx, draw it slowly up the spine. In doing so, let your right hand lie on the coccyx and keep your left hand moving upwards, towards the head, just above the spot where the stagnant energy occurs at the moment. If one region turns out to be particularly resistant, place your right hand just in front of the stagnation point and your left hand exactly over it.

Perhaps it may also be necessary to use fingers only. Place the middle finger of your right hand on the stagnation point and the index finger of your left hand above it. By means of this polarisation, the life energy can slowly form a channel for itself up to the head.

38

The following techniques are also useful for opening the channels of energy.

Photo 38 shows how the skin is rolled upwards to right and left along the spine. During the whole rolling process, your partner should keep all the muscles of his back relaxed. In some regions of the spine the skin can less easily be rolled. Be gentle and kind in all your movements. Do not force the opening of a channel of energy. Sooner or later, with the aid of the flow of life energy, it will open between your hands. Patience and calmness are important aids to polarity balancing.

Photo 39 shows how with light thumb pressure the opening of the energy channel can be assisted.

Should your partner have pain in the spine, or even some abnormalities, advise her to visit an orthopaedic surgeon, a chiropractor or a physiotherapist. Polarity therapy should in no case be used by a layman to correct so-called faulty posture or diseases of the spine. It is the same with polarity therapy as it is with yoga. Both systems can assist in the healing of special disorders and abnormalities, but they are no substitute for medical therapy.

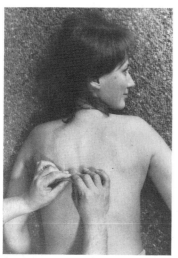

Photo 38: Rolling up the skin near the spine.

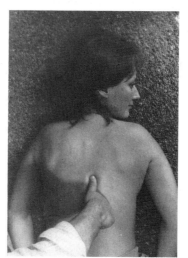

Photo 39: Light pressure with the thumb to left and right along the spine.

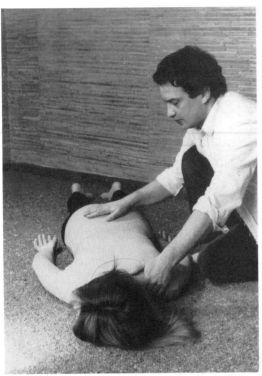

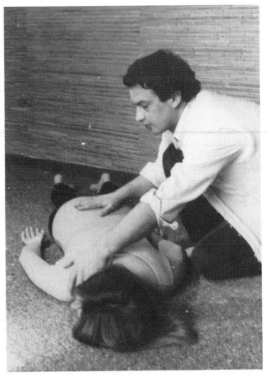

Photo 40: Right hand on the coccyx, left hand on the left shoulder blade.

Photo 41: Right hand on the coccyx, left hand on the right shoulder blade.

The polarity contacts shown in photos 40 and 41 are applicable when the stream of life energy goes off to the left or the right into the shoulder. In the case of deviation to the left, the left hand is placed flat on the right shoulder in order to provide the necessary counterweight for correcting the course of the stream. When the energy deviates to the right, the left hand should be placed on the left shoulder.

Give your partner time to reorientate himself. Do not hurry him. Energy which has deviated for years in a certain channel cannot be restored to its natural course in a very short time.

It may be better for development if the left hand is not placed so high up but is lain on the lower part of the shoulder blade. Concentrate on your partner and let the picture come into your mind of the polarity contact which

40

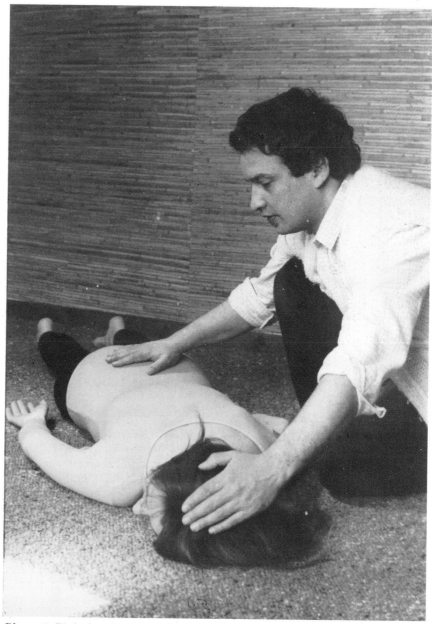

Photo 42: Right hand on the coccyx, left hand on the top of the skull.

will be suitable for the next stage in development. If you empty yourself inwardly and then concentrate and ask what is at that time the best and most useful polarity contact, you will perhaps see it in front of you or know it intuitively.

The three polarity contacts shown on photos 40-42 form the basis of the variations which can be used to restore the life energy to its original and natural course.

The back is often blocked to a large extent, or even entirely, by retained energy. Polarity has many contacts to free it, to drain it away or to direct it to the right place. Basically, with very few exceptions, in polarity the left hand remains above the right, always towards the head, since, as already explained, a person is charged more positively at the head and more negatively at the feet.

Polarity contacts to free the retained energy in the back:
a) Left hand below the left shoulder blade, right hand at the back of the left thigh.
b) Left hand below the right shoulder blade, right hand at the back of the right thigh. It is also possible to place your left hand on either shoulder blade. Try out what seems to you and your partner to be most suitable in any one situation.
c) Your partner lies face downwards. Your left hand is placed at the base of his neck in front, and your right hand on his coccyx.
d) Your partner lies on his right side. You place your left hand between his navel and his solar plexus and your right hand on the nape of his neck.
e) Your partner lies face downwards, with your left hand at the base of his neck. Don't exert any pressure with this hand. Your right hand is placed on his coccyx. With your right hand shake his pelvis to and fro. Take care not to go on shaking after you feel some resistance.
f) Your left hand is placed on the upper part of your partner's shoulder blade. Your right hand lies below the base of the ribs.

Shoulders, neck and arms

The shoulders are a region in which energy is particularly apt to become stuck and from which it is very hard to dislodge this condition. It becomes stuck when a person has something particularly hard to bear and has to protect himself. Overloading occurs through an excess of information, feelings or thoughts. This energy becomes frozen when the person has no possibility of expressing himself verbally or through actions.

The basis of such a block was laid down in early childhood. The person as a young man was not able to master emotionally trying situations, or duties were placed on him which weighed too heavily on his shoulders. If such massive pressure is maintained for a long time, the shoulders will be forced upwards and pulled forwards. As a reaction to a threatening and burdensome situation he is 'frozen' in this position. The result is a crooked back.

Through this posture, movements and feelings from the abdomen and the heart are locked up in the throat below the vocal chords and are thus no longer able to enter into consciousness. The neck is compressed and the nape becomes rigid. In this position the translation of feelings into actions is usually blocked at the collar bone in front of the shoulder joint. Energy for moving the arms is then restricted and too strongly controlled by the head. With some people the arms are separated from the body and of course 'seizing life with both hands' and pursuing it actively is quite impossible without arms!

People without energy in their arms are limited in their self-expression and imprisoned in their narrow world of feeling and experience. To other people they sometimes appear very self-willed.

Exercise: Sit on a chair and relax. Look into yourself with your inner eye and look attentively at the energy picture of the upper part of your back:

> In this part of your body are there any black spots, grey spots or white spots?
> Does life energy flow through the shoulders?

Look at your spine from the height of the shoulders to the beginning of the head:

> Is the energy in the vertebrae more light than dark?
> Are you unable to recognise definite vertebrae?

43

Now look at your shoulder blades.

Are they light rather than dark?

Are light or dark spots recognisable on them or in them?

Are the shoulder blades surrounded by fixed energy?

How is the energy distributed in the upper part of the shoulder?

Is it more inclined to flow or to be stagnant?

Is there a band of energy all round your neck?

Is the energy at the bottom of your neck different from that towards the shoulder blades?

Look at your neck from the point of view of the distribution of energy:

Is there an energy connection between neck and trunk?

Is there any special place where no energy can be seen?

Does the nape of your neck allow enough energy to flowthrough?

Now for the arms. First of all the right side: examine the supply of energy and the state of energy in the shoulder joint.

Does the supply of energy perhaps stop in front of the shoulder joint or behind it?

Is the arm as a whole well supplied with energy or are there weak spots?

Has energy gathered in the elbow or the wrist?

What is the energy connection between the hand and the forearm?

How does the distribution of energy in the hand appear?

Proceed in the same way with your left arm and left hand.

Examine your left arm and hand and compare them with the right.

Are there any basic differences in the structure and distribution of energy? If so, try to find out what causes these differences. If you have answered these questions as far as it is possible at the moment, have another look at the distribution of energy in the arms.

Exercise: Stand upright and spread out your arms to left and right at shoulder height. Let pictures come to you of your arms. Perhaps sentences will come into your mind as well.

44

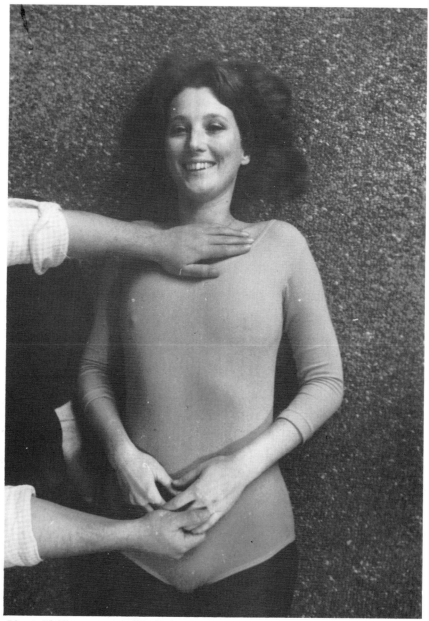

Photo 43: Your partner lies on her back, both her hands placed side by side on her abdomen. Your right hand holds her fingers, your left hand lies on her throat.

Feel that your left hand has a negative charge compared with the right. Be aware of your two hands as opposite poles. Let energy flow between the two poles. Examine the course of the life energy carefully. Look to see whether this horizontal flow of energy is united with the vertical one at the spine.

Drop your arms and see how you feel.

We continually find that after this exercise some become consciously aware of their arms and shoulders for the first time in their lives.

The polarity contact shown in photo 43 combines emotions such as love, acceptance and a feeling of belonging with the means of expression in the hands. Perhaps energy flows less strongly through one arm than through the other.

In order to intensify the flow of energy through the arms, the following polarity contacts may be used (photos 44, 45).

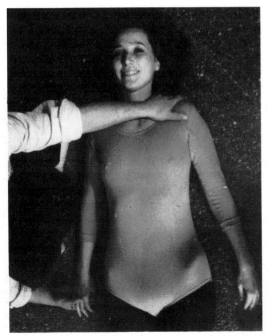 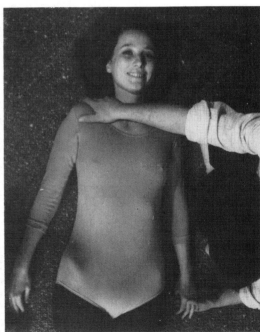

Photo 44: Your partner lies on her back. Your left hand on her left shoulder, your right hand holding the fingers of her right hand.

Photo 45: Your partner lies on her back, your right hand on her right shoulder, your left hand holding the fingers of her left hand.

These polarity contacts seem to contradict the principle that your left hand should be on the right side of your partner and your right hand on her left side. In these contacts you hold the side which has the same polarity as your hand. The explanation for this is simple. The left hand and arm are primarily receptive. Energy flows up the arm into the body and brain. The right hand and arm by contrast are active, rather than receptive. They are instruments for taking action in the world, and to this end energy flows through them from brain and body. In most people the active mode is stronger; they would rather *do* something than merely 'feel' and be passively influenced by events. That is why the energy in the right arm is usually stronger and flows more freely than in the left. Through this polarisation 'the other way round' the flow of energy inwards or outwards, as the case may be, is intensified.

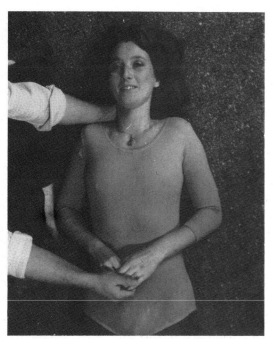

Photo 46: Partner lies on her back, your left hand on the nape of her neck, your right hand holding the fingers of both her hands.

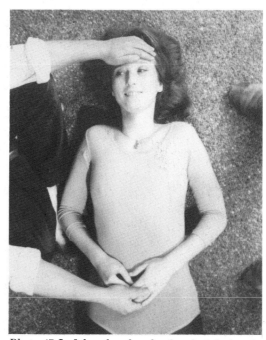

Photo 47: Left hand on her forehead, right hand holding the fingers of both her hands.

47

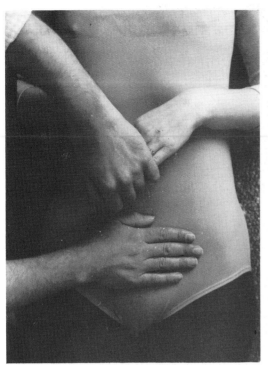

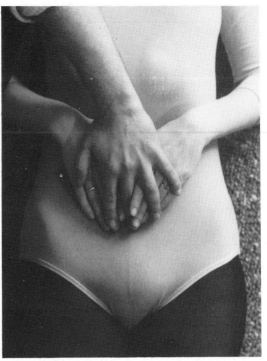

Photo 48: Partner lies on her back, your left hand holding the fingers of both her hands, your right hand on her abdomen above the pubic bone.

Photo 49: Partner lies on her back with her hands on her abdomen. The middle finger of your left hand lies between her hands, touching both of them. Your thumb and index finger touch her right hand and your third and little finger touch her left hand.

Sometimes, in order to unblock the energy channel, it may be necessary to take your partner's left hand in your right hand and place your left hand on his right shoulder. In order to polarise the right arm the opposite will of course hold good.

Photo 46 shows how the vital energy in the neck, shoulders, arms and hands can all be connected up. Retained energy can then flow down the arms and out through the hands, thus enabling a new flow to begin. The connection between the neck and the hands has the further effect of harmonsing deliberate action.

Photo 47 shows how a connection is made between thought and action. The energy of thought is no longer shut up in the head, but can now be changed into action.

48

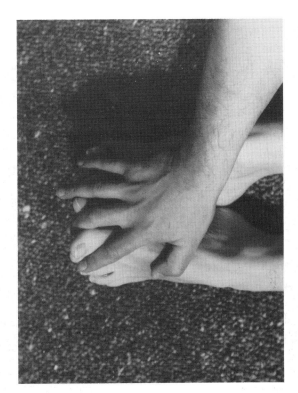

Photo 50: Partner lies with feet together. The middle finger of your right hand lies between her feet, touching both of them. Your thumb and index finger touch her left foot, and your third and little fingers touch her right foot.

The action will be better thought out because there is now no longer any block between the organs of thought and action.

Photo 48 shows the opening of a channel to the hands for the feelings arising in the abdomen, which can then be transformed through this polarisation. The energy flows through the whole front of the body and activates it. Blocks in the region of the abdomen and chest are lessened and become less impermeable.

If the connection between the hands and feet is sufficiently established, then that person will be better adapted to life. He will be more capable of action and will proceed more in harmony with the life force.

The vital energy flows from the feet through the leg, through the pelvis and back and over the shoulders through the arms to the hands.

49

If the connection between head and body is established, then all parts of the body will be connected energetically with one another. It is then that many people for the first time experience their own wholeness. This wholeness is a higher level of energy, and greater vitality is accompanied by increased calmness. Movements become more graceful and rounded. One's self-respect and love of oneself and one's fellow humans is increased.

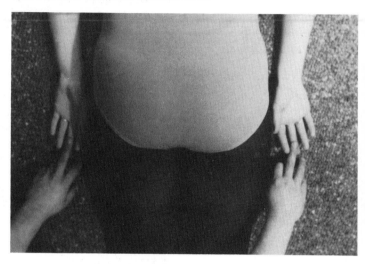

Photo 51: Partner lying face downwards, arms at her sides, palms upwards. The middle finger of your left hand is on the middle finger of her left hand, the middle finger of your right hand on the middle finger of her right hand.

Through this polarity contact (photo 51) the vital energy flowing along the spine is connected with the vital energy in the arms. At the same time the energy of the two arms merges at the shoulders.

A possible variation consists in putting your left hand on your partner's spine, just below the point where her neck begins, and your right hand on her right hand. In this way you can establish or strengthen the connection with her right hand.

In order to do the same for her left hand or arm, place your right hand on her spine at the point described above and your left hand on her palm.

There are additional polarity contacts which increase vital energy in the region of the shoulders and the nape of the neck. In the first you place your right hand on your partner's shoulder at the nape of the neck and your left hand on the back of her head. Your partner should be lying on her stomach with her face towards you, and you should be on the left side of her body.

You stand behind your partner and place your right hand on her right shoulder and your left hand on the left side of her head, above the ear.

Conversely, place your left hand on her left shoulder and your right hand on the upper part of her head above the ear.

Stand in front of your partner and place your left hand sideways on her right shoulder joint and your right hand on the left shoulder joint. Often this will enable the energy in the shoulders to flow through for the first time.

If blocks in the neck, shoulders, arms and hands are removed, the vitality, the life energy slumbering in the pelvis will rise and can be converted into creativity, joie de vivre, harmony, contentment, love for one's fellows, and composure. Someone whose shoulders have been freed can no longer be oppressed by anything, because he can immediately act and react in tune with his own individuality. People at this stage of development are scarcely able any longer to distinguish between action and reaction, since these two polarities have become a unity. Their action, their thought and their feelings have become one with their vital energy.

The Head

The head is the highest member of a person's body. It is, so to speak, enthroned above everything else. Inside the head is the central switchboard, the brain. The sensors for tasting, hearing, smelling and seeing are located here. The senses are not far from their centre. In the midddle of the head is the pituitary gland, which controls and regulates secretions of the body.

The head may be compared to the king of a country. If he is a tyrant he will rule his land (the body) with an iron hand and exploit it, making impossible demands upon it. He distances himself from his people, despising them because they are subordinate to him. As a despot he will issue senseless commands and will seek to make war at the expense of his own country in order to become ever more powerful. A tyrant like that asserts that he is far-sighted and can make the right decisions at all times. He is a law-giver and judge combined. He will assert that he stands for high ideals (religion, the state, morals etc.). The result of such domination is that the people remain immature, unconscious, cut off from the rest of the world.

However, the oppressed people try again and again to get rid of these tyrants by rebelling. So too with the body. Illness breaks out. The head is brought down. It must lie down in bed!

People with tyrant heads have their heads separated from their bodies. The head has its own life. This is the 'real' life: the rest of the body must do as it is told. Bodily rebellion in the form of depression, fear, aversions or neurosis is soon, however, put down. The pharmaceutical industry has many weapons in readiness.

In addition to the tyrant type there is also the wise ruler. He knows all about the movements and moods in his kingdom. He is in communication with all parts of his land. He, too, exercises the power of a ruler, but always with discretion, with wisdom, and for the good of the whole commumity. He places his knowledge at the disposal of the kingdom as a whole and its individual parts, ensuring what is to everyone's advantage; for a wise king rules by serving others.

These two types of rulers illustrate the basic ways in which the head is, or is not, connected to the body.

People with the head of a tyrant seem to be all head. Their problems, the way they associate with other people, their attitude towards nature, the way they walk, their sex life: in a word everything is 'done' with the head. Most politicians belong to this type. They view the needs of other people with the irrational logic of the conference table. Feelings are thought through with the head and programmed according to the effect they will have. For this reason wrong decisions are unavoidable. If the head has no connection with the body, it will be cold and objective, calculating, heartless, 'withdrawn'. We live in a society where the head predominates, in which everything is recorded and arranged with expert clarity. The wonder child of this society is the computer.

What becomes so strikingly evident in the sphere of politics and society is only a large scale indication of what the individual members of this society are like: beings who are just heads alienated from their bodies. Only those feelings may be shown which are sanctioned by reason; other feelings are blocked off and not allowed to penetrate the consciousness. We know only too well what the results of this has been. both on the individual and on collective

52

life. In the same way that we maltreat animals, we maltreat our own feelings. In the same way that we see our fellow humans, we see ourselves. Only when we ourselves – each one of us – can find the way to unity and wholeness, can the world about us become whole again. Inner and outer worlds correspond, down to the smallest detail.

In the meantime there is a widespread counter-movement. People are trying to 'find their bodies again' and to see themselves and their fellow humans as whole people. A very large-scale adjustment is taking place in our culture. It is the law of polarity: if the pendulum swings in one direction, then it will certainly swing back in the other direction. The strong tendency of the last two hundred years towards rationality is about to find its counterpart. The inwardness and spirituality of the East is approaching, although not without difficulty, a fruitful union with the rationality of the West. Buddhist centres are springing up all over the world. Eastern medicine (e.g. acupuncture) is finding entry into western technical knowledge. Both hemispheres, East and West are learning from each other. Each has reached the end of its own particular development. Each side is becoming richer in itself through opening up to the opposite pole. It is time for humanity to overcome all opposition which causes separation, in order that it may survive.

Each time that opposition is overcome is a step towards the perfection of the individual and of humankind as a whole.

Polarity is also part of an East-West exchange. We Westerners are beginning to make use for our inward and outward development of the knowledge which has grown up over the centures about the polarities of yin and yang. As a matter of fact, we in the West have already in our own way recognised the yin-yang principle, and we have been using it for a long time now, for example in electricity. We have only to insert a plug into a wall socket for the interplay of plus and minus to lighten much of our work. The potential difference between the plus and minus poles generates a force which is effective in a wholly concrete sense.

When head and body are working together, the wisdom of the body comes into communication with the knowledge of the head. The result is a new, yet old, unity, which is much more vital and true to life than the well-known, but very ineffective, duality of head versus body.

The whole of evolution has only one goal: complete human beings.

Exercise: Sit on a chair with your back straight. Be aware of your coccyx and your head as polarities. Allow energy to flow between the two poles. Observe it flowing, but don't interfere.

Now stand up. Be aware of your feet and your head as polarities. Allow energy to flow between the two poles as well. Observe where the flow is interrupted, where it becomes slower and weaker. Observe, but don't make a value judgement! If you make a value judgement you have again fallen into the trap of reason. The life force recognises neither 'good' nor 'bad'.

The head is the seat of important sense organs: the tongue, the eyes, the ears, the nose. They are important means of communication. Probably each one of us will have trouble with these organs in the head. Sometimes we will have had a sluggish or dirty tongue, our eyes will have been dim, our nose or ears blocked. Troubles can also be seen as the result of energy blocks in these regions.

Many people have also got bogged down in their brains through retained energy. Something has 'gone to their heads'. Many a person goes about brooding heavily or his thoughts go round in a circle – his head is going 'round and round'. There are many telling expressions in the vernacular for energy blocks in the region of the head: stiff-necked, thick-witted. etc.

With us in the West the head is a member very prone to disturbance, because we present it with problems which it can solve only with difficulty or not at all. We try to understand another thing which would be better felt. We try to listen to something else when we should do better just to go along with it. We try to think something out which we could more easily understand intuitively.

Take a look at your life from the point of view of the misapplication of such functions. It is enlightening to talk about this with a partner or friend, since we have often through custom become blind to such misapplications.

A region very susceptible to retained energies is the part round the occipital bone at the back or the skull.

Exercise: Your partner lies on his or her back. Massage and press the skin and the muscles below these bones. Hold

Photo 52: Your left hand holds the head, your right hand massages the occipital bone.

his head with your left hand and with your right hand massage and knead lightly on the right side of the back of his head. In order to massage the other side, take his head in your hand and work with your left. Let yourself be guided by the life force about how long and how intensively you work. It will convey to you a sense of the right timing. Stroke the released energy over the shoulders and down to the hands.

Exercise: Facial massage always gives a pleasant sensation. It is a pleasure to see how your partner relaxes before your very eyes, and how many bodily energies are restored to their right proportions through this massage. The partner lies on her back and the masseur kneels behind her head. It is important for the masseur to have warm hands. Before starting, visualise the following picture: yuour partner's whole body is represented in her face. Her head is above the root of the nose on the forehead. Her neck corresponds to the root of the nose. Her shoulders may be found in her eyebrows. Her arms run from the end of her eyebrows over her cheeks to the middle of her jaw muscles, where her hands have their corresponding place. Her body is represented by her nose. The sex organs are between her nose and her upper lip. Her legs run down from her nostrils, her knees being about the height of the corner of her mouth and her shins running down from there to the hollow above her chin, a quarter of an inch below the middle of his lower lip. Her legs lie together in the middle of her chin. Make a point of beginning the massage at the root of the nose; this is her 'body'. You will observe that in the case of the more fully conscious people, parts of the body can be well relaxed by massaging the corresponding parts of the face. A single facial massage can relax a person completely, but it is important that this massage should begin with the root of the nose.

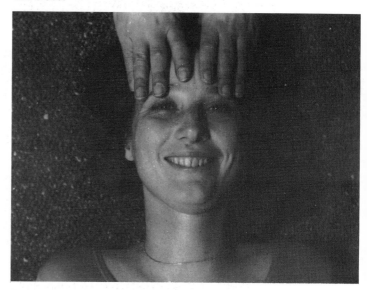

Photo 53: Partner lying down. Your thumbs, pointing downwards, lie on her head. Your fingers massage her forehead.

Lay your thumbs on the crown of your partner's head, so that they do not touch, and stroke with your fingers over the forehead. This polarity contact can 'open' your partner's head if he or she is ready for it.

Many people have a scarcely noticeable, but almost perpetual slight pressure under the scalp. This energy can then be released and such a release brings greater consciousness.

With the polarity contact shown on photo 54, the entire energy of the region of the head can begin to flow., Retained energy is set in motion around the occipital bone, in the pharynx, in the teeth, in and behind the eyes and in the front part of the brain. This contact is best made after

56

Photo 54: Your right hand at the base of the occipital bone, your left hand in front of your partner's forehead.

Photo 55: Your right hand under the chin, left hand at the back of the head in the middle.

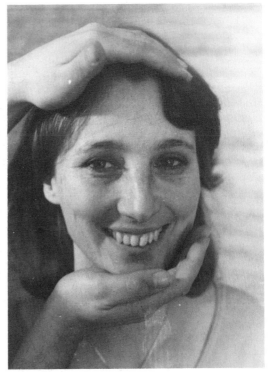

Photo 56: Your right hand on the back of the head, your left hand on the forehead in the direction of the root of the nose.

Photo 57: Your right hand under the chin, your left hand on the crown of your partner's head, slightly to the front.

massaging over the occipital bone. It is particularly effective when used for a short while two or three times a week. The arrested thought 'structures' can then slowly be freed. Thought which has become stuck fast appears to the inward eye like granite in the head. This granite should be dissolved slowly and not blown up all at once as if by dynamite.

Superficial, trivial thinking, the uncontrolled thoughts which come into one's mind, can be banished by means of the flow of energy between your hands. In this kind of stagnation of energy a person is forced into dwelling on trivialities. In this condition there can be no true meeting of person to person, heart to heart, nor can there be a true dialogue between people or the discussion of common problems.

59

Photo 58: Partner lying on her face. Your left hand on the back of her head, your right hand in the middle of her back on the spine.

The following polarity contact can free the mind of superfluous ballast and set free the potential for true analysis and constructive thought:

By means of the flow which arises between the poles, the upper region of your partner's head is freed from retained energies. In addition, part of the rigid energy behind the eyes is set in motion.

The masks which people wear with others are in and on their faces. Their masks arise through energy blocks which occur all over the face and which work together. One's 'true face' is hidden behind them. Actually there is no *one* true face, for being without a mask means that the human face will have a multipicity of possibilities of expression. Some well-known masks are: the depressive expression, the poker face, the keep-smiling, the clown, the outraged beauty, the expressionless expression, etc. A person shows his momentary identity, but not his individuality. Most people are so firmly frozen into their mask that they are no longer conscious of who is wearing it.

Exercise: Stand in front of a mirror and look yourself in the face. Can you recognise a permanent mask?

Touch your face. Can you feel your muscles tensed to a greater or lesser extent?

Try out a new face in front of the mirror. Put on one face after another. Get to know your facial masks!

What is your real, individual face? Can you find it?

Keep on trying out 'your' faces, so that you develop a consciousness of facial expression.

Vital energy streams through the face. At first, if the masks are very firmly fixed, the energy only streams over the skin, but it will find its own way in through different layers of tissue. Chronic retained energy in the teeth, the nose, the nasal cavity, the eyes and the frontal cavity is released. This results in the relaxation of all facial muscles. A person then has more possibilities of self-expression by means of the face.

A block is usually to be found round the mouth, right round the lips. The flow of vital energy through the face helps to lessen and remove this 'lock jaw'. There is a connection between the energising round the mouth and round the genitals. Both circles are involved in a ban on the enjoyment of certain parts of life.

60

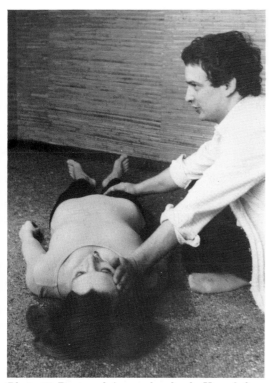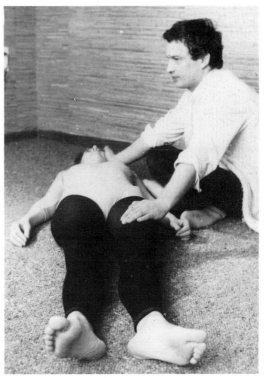

Photo 59: Partner lying on her back. Your left hand on the right half of her head, your right hand on her left thigh.

Photo 60: Your right hand on the left half of the head, your left hand on the left thigh.

The polarity contact shown above allows energy to flow through the nape of the neck, and removes blocks at the occipital bone. Energies which have 'solidified' and become stuck there on account of psychic pressures on the neck are released. The nape of the neck can readjust and become more flexible. Those whose necks are flexible suffer much less than other people from headaches.

A variation of this contact consists in placing your right hand on the spine between the shoulder blades, and your left hand on the forehead. Try out the effects of these contacts yourself.

The polarity contacts depicted on plates 59 and 60 show head and legs are connected with one another. the energy flows down over the front part of the body.

If it is required to establish this connection in the back

part of the body, your partner will lie face downwards. Your left hand lies on the back of the right thigh and your right hand on the left half of the head.

After that, you place your left hand on the left side of the head and your right hand on the back of the left thigh. This makes energy flow through the buttocks, the back and the nape of the neck to the head.

The left half of the brain is more concerned with action. The right hand is inclined towards receptivity. Thus the left half of the brain is connected with the right hand and the right half with the left hand.

By means of these polarity contacts the connection between the respective corresponding parts will be established or strengthened.

Photo 60: Your right hand lies on the left half of the head, your left hand holds your partner's right hand.

Photo 61: Your left hand lies on the right half of the head, your right hand holds your partner's left hand.

3. The Chakras

The word 'chakra' comes from the Sanskrit and means 'wheel', because the chakra is a circular centre of spiralling energy. In the East they are also thought of as lotus blossoms, with petals partly or wholly open or closed. The condition of one of these chakras or of the chakras in general shows a person's stage of development in one special region, or overall. In a less developed person the chakras will glow with only slight intensity or they may be closed up altogether. In the case of a more fully developed person, a chakra will send out pulsating and vital beams of energy far beyond the body. There are various assertions about the positions and function of the chakras, some authors basing their version on three chakras, others on seven, nine or eleven. I have discovered that chakras with similar functions are to be found in different parts of the body, but it is not clear whether some of them have 'wandered' or whether they have been in that place from birth. It is, however, relatively easy to discover where a half-open chakra is to be found.

Photo 63: Partner lying on her back, your left hand over her abdomen.

Exercise: Your partner is lying on her back. You are on her left or right side. Your left hand glides at a height of about an inch above the middle of her abdomen. In some places you will feel in your hand a slight tingling, a sensation of warmth of a current of energy coming from your partner. This current is most easily found just below the navel or in the region of the solar plexus.

Now with your left hand try to find further points of energy in the middle of your partner's body. Sometimes the current of energy will be almost imperceptible. In that case let your hand rest there, and in short while the current of energy will be strengthened; then move your hand a little higher up, so that you maintain gentle contact with the energy.

The Position of the Chakras

The chakras are most likely to be found at the following points in the body:

> The first chakra at the lower end of the spine in men and between the ovaries in women.
> The second chakra below the navel.
> The third chakra at the solar plexus.
> The fourth chakra in the middle of the chest.
> The fifth chakra in the larynx.
> The sixth chakra above the root of the nose.
> The seventh chakra at the top of the head.
> There may also be a chakra in each hand and in each foot.

The first chakra (the root chakra) has the function of establishing harmony with the earth. In addition it regulates the survival mechanism. If someone is in a situation where his life is at risk, this chakra will increase its activity, forcing the person in question to focus his whole attention on preserving the basic functions of life. A healthy root chakra ensures the best chances of survival under all conditions. A part of human survival is the possibility of reproduction, so this first chakra is also responsible for regulating the sex organs. If this chakra is incapable of fully functioning, the person concerned will be depressed and scarcely in a position to look after himself. Those with healthy sexuality are capable in life and those with impaired sexuality always have difficulty in protecting their lives. If the root chakra is perpetually closed up, that person will lose his connection with the world around him and will land in inward and outward chaos. He/she is at odds with the conditions in which (s)he lives. He develops his own peculiar view of 'reality' and usually acts in an inappropriate way towards the world around him. This is inevitable, because connection with the world outside through the first chakra is blocked and so (s)he does not possess the correct information on which to base his actions.

The second chakra – the so-called vitality chakra – is found a little below the navel. It is with the help of this chakra that we establish physical and mental stabilty. Someone with a healthy vitality chakra is safe within himself as if he were 'in Abraham's bosom'. Also with the help of this chakra we become aware of some of the feelings of our fellow human beings. It also regulates our erotic sensibility to some extent and helps in choosing a partner. If someone's vitality chakra is not functioning properly, this will bring many unpleasant results. (S)he will feel out of contact. He will not be sufficiently sensitive to the feelings of his fellow beings and will feel himself cut off from them. The only power on which he can draw lies within himself, which means that he will soon be exhausted.

The third chakra, the spleen chakra, is the centre from which psychic and physical energies are distributed. A spleen chakra which is working harmoniously enables a person to be active psychically and physically at the right moment. This does not mean that such a person may not sometimes experience difficulties in completing his actions. The reason for this would be as yet unresolved blocks in the region of the extremities. A spleen chakra which is working properly brings with it the potential for spiritual and physical harmony. If anyone experiences fear, a feeling we all know, then his possibility of action is limited – a 'sinking feeling in the stomach' renders him incapable of it. If the spleen chakra is permanently closed, frenzy which cannot be got rid of will build up in the stomach region. In spite of potentially great power, a person then feels powerless, uneasy, hemmed in. If he observes his movements, he will discover that they are not harmonious. Power is stuck in the abdomen and cannot find its way into the limbs.

The three lower chakras, the root, vitality and spleen chakras, are concerned with the regulation of our existential needs.

Many people come together in self-realisation groups, hoping, though this is usually not explicit, to 'develop spiritually'. This desire is, however, often a sign that the 'lower material' needs have not been sufficiently satisfied. Many even try by means of spiritual development to avoid confronting the 'lower' region and effecting a change in it. The result is that the body becomes more and more denied and the duality of body and mind which is already present is thereby strengthened even further. In consequence such a person becomes ever less successful in life. In spite of higher spiritual development, he retains a generalised and diffuse fear of life, perhaps awkward and uncertain behaviour, sexual difficulties and a latent rejection of his own foundation as a skyscraper built on sand.

The fourth chakra, the heart chakra, is responsible for harmonising energy in the chest region. A person in whom this chakra is working well is a 'heart person', a loving one. He is open to the needs and vibrations of the world around him. His heart beats for humankind and all creation. He loves himself. But if the heart chakra is closed, a loving exchange is no longer possible. Most people in whom such a condition exists have experienced little or no love in their lives, especially when they were children. The chakra closed up when their love was not returned. The result of this is often inner loneliness, the feeling of having been abandoned and frequently lasting difficulties in partnerships. Further results are extreme introversion, attachment to sentimentality and to material goods. Mid-European society consists mostly of people with closed hearts. There is scarcely any cordial exchange of goods, feelings or words.

The fifth chakra is the one concerned with individuality, and harmonises communication and the ability of the individual to express himself. If this chakra is closed, then individuality cannot find expression in the voice and in the movement of the upper extremities. Such people do not know who they really are: they have not discovered their own individuality. Instead they live only through identification. They are present in themselves and creative on their own account. In our culture closed heart and neck chakras are the general rule. It has become a widespread custom not to open one's heart chakra and not to reveal oneself.

The sixth chakra, on the forehead, provides an overall perspective. We all know people with closed forehead chakras: they have lost this overall perspective. This loss is often accompanied be slight pressure or by headache. An open 'third eye' permits greater far-sightedness and heightened ability to know oneself. A person with an open 'third eye' can look at the essence of things and it can even be useful in such a mundane task as looking for a place to park! Besides that, it enables one to make better use of one's time.

The seventh chakra, the crown, strives for an even greater extension of consciousness. It is the crown of man or woman. If it is open, it is the door to all-embracing knowledge. Through the vital energy working in this chakra a person becomes permanently unified and is led to

66

an ever greater revelation of his own being.
Through exercise comes experience,
Through experience comes knowledge,
After knowledge comes intuition,
After intuition comes direct action.

Deviations from the Normal Condition

The chakras can show various kinds of deviation from the normal condition. They may have too little energy to fulfil their functions, but they may also be overcharged with energy. Chakras may be broken permanently closed or spoiled. They may also be cut off from vital energy in the back.

Photo 64 gives a representation of the energy of a healthy chakra seen from the side. It is connected with the vital energy in the back by means of a stalk and opens out in front like a calyx.

Overcharged chakras are usually surrounded by a cloud of darker energy at the calyx. Undercharged chakras appear thin and emaciated, as though they were under-nourished. A chakra becomes overcharged when a person tries to solve with his brain questions which should really be solved, for example, with the help of the vitality chakra. If the overcharging lasts for any length of time, the energy of the vitality chakra becomes diverted into the head towards the forehead and becomes lodged there. It will be the cause of chronic mental disturbance and chronic lack of vitality.

Broken chakras are those which have completely lost their function. The causes of this are traumatic experiences which made such a strong impression on the functional region of the chakra that it broke.

Dirty chakras are filled up with retained energy. This causes the flow of energy between inside the person and the environment to be effective only in certain sections. The incoming and outgoing information is only partial and is therefore imperfect.

Chronically closed chakras are the chief source of trouble. It is exactly as if such a chakra were not there at all. A person is in this respect closed up.

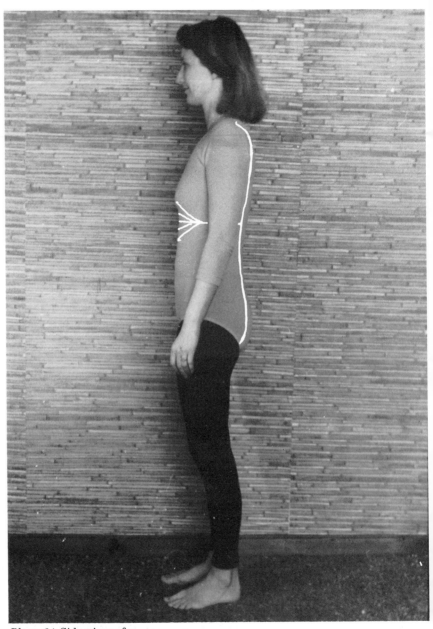

Photo 64: Side view of a
healthy chakra

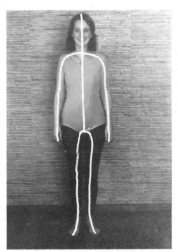

Photo 65: Upright position. The line indicates energy flow.

Besides the seven main chakras, there are four secondary chakras in the hands and feet.

The chakra in the right hand is responsible for regulating the outward flow of energy. If the discharge of energy or the chakra itself becomes impaired through some block or other, then that person is not able to act correctly. The left hand chakra regulates the intake of energy from the environment, and with this intake, certain information; feeling and sensations are also absorbed and registered internally. If this chakra is unable to function fully, the person will have difficulty in receiving impulses from the world outside in the proper way. The two hand chakras are particularly important for our polarity work, since the positively and negatively charged currents (right and left) flow through them.

Exercise: Hold your hands in front of your chest so that the palms are facing one another a little way apart and let the energy flow between them. Be aware of the chakras in the palms of the left and right hands. Now half close the hands and open them completely again. You will observe that through the opening and closing of the chakras the flow of energy is increased and diminished.

The two foot chakras (on the insteps) regulate the exchange of energy between man/woman and the earth, in the same way that the hand chakras control it between man/woman and the environment. All chakras should be connected with the vital energy flowing in the back through the spine.

Exercise: Visualise your chakras, one by one, starting from the vitality chakra. You can consider chakras according to the criteria described above, but you can also experience the energy they manifest. How do they *feel*? Observe, but do not make a value judgement.

Exercise: Observe the chakra in your right foot. Let it open a little at first, then half way, then fully. Feel what has changed. Now open the chakra of your left foot as well. What has changed in the way you feel? Open it or close it to whatever extent makes you feel well. Do the same with the other nine chakras. It is unwise to have all your chakras open for long, as you can become quite vulnerable.

If you repeat this exercise frequently you will in time acquire a better sense of these energy regulators and will know when to leave the correct chakras open and when to close them in certain situations.

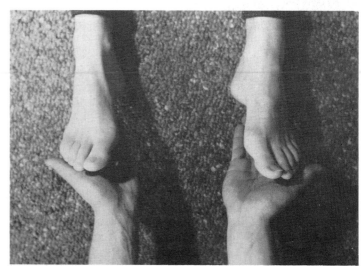

Photo 66: Partner lying on back, your right hand an inch below the sole of the right foot your left hand below the sole of the right foot at the same distance.

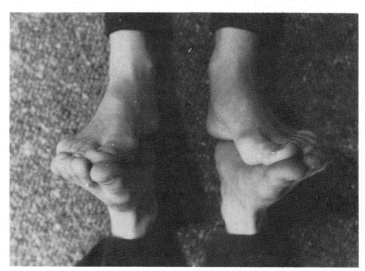

Photo 67: Partners lying on their backs with the soles of their feet touching.

Photo 68: Your right hand at the nape of the neck, your left hand on the larynx.

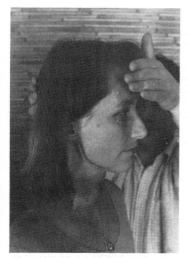

Photo 69: Your right hand at the back of the head, your left hand just in front of the forehead.

Work on the Chakras

If the work of the chakras has been upset, polarity balancing can put it right again. Do not begin this kind of polarity work until the flow of vital energy in the back is strong enough to be connected with a chakra. If the vital energy in the back flows only as far as the spleen chakra, you should work only in the lower three chakras. The vital energy must flow right up to the heart chakra if you are to be able to establish a significant connection there. In polarity work we move through the chakras from the bottom upwards.

Both exercises help clear the foot chakras, to open them and, if necessary, to adjust them. The exercise shown on photo 66 is particularly suitable for polarity work with one person and the exercise shown on photo 67 for groups.

Exercise: Observe the condition of each of your partner's chakras. You may, for example, see that the lower chakras are healthy, but that the heart chakra is closed. In that case, pay attention to the course of the vital energy in the back, seeing if it runs up to the level of the chakra, and if it is weakened at the point where the stalk of the chakra should connect with it. If that is the case, work first on strengthening and stabilising the energy in the back. When you have done this, lay your right hand between your partner's shoulder blades at the place where the stalk of the chakra should connect with it. Place your left hand on the chest at the place where the calyx is, or where it should be. Look carefully now with your inner eye to see how the energy is flowing. Sometimes at first no stream of energy is visible. It takes time for the vital energy to work its way through the many blocks. 'Solid' energy is often like a heavy and massive lump of lead stuck in the chest. Chakras which have been deformed or closed for years cannot be 'repaired' in a short time. Remain attentive and let yourself be guided by your hands. A partner who has been living for a considerable time with an unhealthy chakra must have time to adapt to the healing process.

71

Photo 70: Your right hand on the occipital bone, your left hand on the crown of the head. By means of this polarity contact the crown chakra can be purified. The weight of obstructing thought, which is present in most people, is thereby removed and when it has gone objective thinking can begin.

Work on the neck chakra should proceed in conjunction with the balancing of the whole shoulder, nape of the neck and arm region. If the channels of vital energy are not sufficiently stable in these part of the body, then there is no basis for balancing the fifth chakra. Complete re-establishment of functional capacity in the forehead chakra is connected with ridding the head of retained energy. This can be a lengthy process, since the healing energy between your hands will first run right round the head above the scalp before it finds its way inside. The head is too full, filled up with circling thoughts and age-old mental images. These distort the person's view of the present, making him brood on the future or the past, with thoughts leading to depression or illness. Cleansing the head of retained mental energy usually takes several weeks, since many cherished and accustomed ideas and mental images will have to be relinquished.

Balancing the Energies of the Chakras

Exercise: Partner lying on back. Examine closely the distribution of energy in the chakras. Let what you see have its effect on you without worrying about it. Ask yourself how the energies should be balanced, both singly and in relation to one another. *The answer lies in your hands.* Let yourself be guided by them to the chakras which should be balanced, by means of the vital energy between the hands. The intrinsic wisdom of your hands knows, too, how long the polarity contact should be maintained. It indicates to you whether you should place your hands directly on the body, an inch or two above it, or a foot above the region of the chakra.

Photo 71: Your right hand on the crown chakra, your left hand on the spleen chakra.

Examples of polarity contacts for balancing the chakras are:

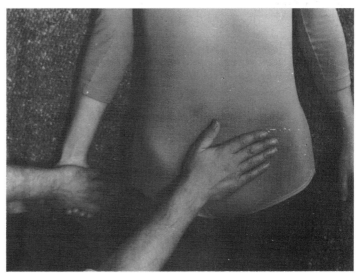

Photo 72: Your left hand in your partner's right hand, your right hand on the second chakra.

Note: All Chakras can be balanced in relation to each other.

In photo 71, the superfluous, retained energy of the crown chakra is conducted back to its place of origin, the spleen chakra.

Photo 72 shows how retained energy in the vitality chakra is conducted into the chakra of the right hand.

73

4. Polarity Exercises

Perception of Polarities

Exercises: Perceive each item in the list below as the polarity of the corresponding item in the opposite column. This exercise is useful in making you aware of polarities which need to be balanced:

left leg	right arm
right leg	left arm
upper part of the body	lower part of the body
left half of the body	right half of the body
coccyx	head
feet	pelvis
body	spirit
chest and abdomen	back
right hand	left hand
legs	arms
neck	nape of the neck
head	body
left ear	right ear
genitals	body
retained energy	flowing energy
I	Thou
I	the space I occupy
I	nature
I	the earth
I	the sun
I	the universe
be air	be earth
be water	be fire
be fire, water, earth, air be circle	be square
be energy	be non-energy
be what you are	be what you are not

You will observe that it is easier for you to perceive unity in some polarities than in others. It is helpful to repeat these exercises over and over again.

Exercise: Select an object and place it in front of you. (It should if possible be made of natural material.) Concentrate on it. Perceive it as polarity to yourself. Let energy flow between you.

Exercise: Ask some other person to do the following exercise with you. Stand facing each other, about four to six feet apart. Look at each other for a while, then shut your eyes and concentrate on each other. Each perceives the other as polar to himself. Let energy flow between you. Repeat this exercise and observe how the connection between you develops.

Exercise: Kneel down, bending forward until your forehead touches the ground. Place your arms beside your head. Let go completely and empty yourself. When you are completely empty, get up, stretch your arms up to the sky and let yourself be filled by energy coming from above. Empty and fill yourself at least seven times running. Decide whether you will end the exercise when you are empty or full. Perceive to the full the difference between the empty and full polarities.

Exercise: Stand up. Take care that your weight is evenly distributed on both feet. Then by means of energy through the legs and feet make a connection with the earth and its centre. Let the connection be formed from the second chakra to the first chakra, so that you are earthed also by means of this chakra. Connect up all the chakras with each other in this way. From the neck chakra let energy flow down into the earth through the arms and hands. If connection has been made with the crown chakra, let the beam of energy go on to the sun and flow into it.

Exercise: Stand up. Hold both arms stretched out in front of your chest. Open your arms, breathing in as you do so. When they are parallel with your shoulders, let them fall to your sides and rest. When breathing in think, and form the words, 'I am opening myself', and when breathing out 'I am present in myself'. Let breathing, movement and speech all be in harmony with each other.

Exercise: Sit cross-legged on the ground with your back straight. If necessary, sit on a cushion. Let your hands rest together in your lap, palms upwards. Now, starting at the coccyx, circle round with your pelvis, back and head. Make the circles larger, then smaller, until finally you stop moving altogether. Come to rest at the centre. Enjoy it!

Exercise: Stand with your knees turned slightly outwards, your hands lying on the lower part of the abdomen. Breathe long, calm breaths in the region of the abdomen where your hands are lying. When it becomes warm inside your abdomen, take your hands away and let a movement begin in the abdomen which will in time embrace the whole body. After about twenty minutes, let the movement subside and rest.

Exercise: Stand up and rock your body forwards and backwards, and from left to right, in any order you like. In this exercise take care to maintain good contact with the ground.

Exercise: Place hands together in front of your chest in the attitude of prayer. Breathe in, pressing your hands together. Breathe out, with your hands lightly touching.

Exercise: Place your hands together in front of your chest in the attitude of prayer. Breath in: press your right hand against the left. Breathe out. Pause. Breathe in: press your left hand against the right. Breathe out. Pause.

Carry out the two hand exercises for about ten minutes.

Exercise: Two partners sit cross-legged opposite each other, placing their hands together, their knees touching lightly. While doing so, they look each other in the eyes and keep silent.

This exercise serves to establish contact and heighten the flow of energy between two people.

Exercise: The two partners stand opposite each other, each one putting his right hand on the other's left shoulder. The left forearms are together in the middle at chest height, with the left hand holding the partner's elbow. Both partners move their left arms first towards their partner and then towards themselves. Notice what happens. Is the yin-yang relationship balanced in these movements or are there blocks which disturb the harmony?

Repeat the exercise with the other arm. In this case, the left hands are on the right shoulders and the right hands and elbows are in the centre.

This exercise reproduces the form of the yin-yang symbol. First the yin force is more strongly marked, then, as a result, the yang force.

Exercise: The partners stand opposite each other, with hands at chest height touching palm to palm. The two pairs of thumbs, index fingers, middle fingers, third fingers and little fingers press against each other in turn, beginning with the thumbs, resulting in a wave-like movement. Then repeat the exercise, beginning with pressure of the little fingers.

Exercise: Partner lying downwards. Look at his back. You will notice that when he is breathing in and out, certain parts of his back will move. Place your hands there. Ask your partner to breathe into these parts. This will produce a feeling of warmth beneath your hands. If it is sufficiently strong, move your hands on half a hand's breadth towards the head. Your partner breathes afresh towards this part. If warmth is produced here too, move your hands on again. In this way, the back including the shoulders, can obtain a better supply of energy. Do not stop the exercise until your hands have rested on every part of the back.

Variation: Stand behind your partner, who is also standing. Place your hands on his shoulders and let him breathe towards your hands. Move your hands over the whole region of the shoulders and nape of the neck.

Exercise: Both partners sit with backs together in such a way that their pelvises, spines, shoulders and the backs of their heads are all just touching. Take care that neither of you is leaning or actually pushing against the other. Consciously feel your back and the energy flowing there. Let the energies of the two backs combine with each other.

Exercise: One partner lies on his back. The other massages the whole region of the abdomen with light clockwise movements.

Exercise: One partner lies on his face. The other massages the back of the pelvic girdle above the coccyx with the ball of his right hand, again in a clockwise direction. Large, slow circling movements produce a pleasant sensation. This massage, like the abdominal massage, can also be carried out on oneself. In this case for the abdominal massage, kneel down, relax the muscles of the abdomen and massage in a clockwise direction up the right side of the abdomen and down the left side. To massage the back of your pelvic girdle, clench your right fist and massage in a clockwise direction with the flat of your thumb and index finger.

Exercise: One partner lies on his right side, the other on his left side, so that the head of each is an arm's length from the feet of the other. The energy circuit is closed. This exercise can also be performed by several people.

Threesome exercises: One person lies on his back on the ground. The second holds the head with his hands, his thumbs behind the ears and his fingers with their tips above the occipital bone. The third partner in the exercise sits at the feet, holding the left leg above the ankle with his right hand, and the right leg above the ankle with his left hand. Energy flows right through the person who is lying down, purifying and relaxing him.

Variation: The partner at the head touches the spine below the seventh cervical vertebra (it stands out a little at the bottom of the neck).

Polarity Circuit according to Richard Gordon

For this, it is necessary to have six masseurs. The first holds the head lightly between his hands. His index and middle fingers point towards the neck, his thumb lies over the ear. The second is on the right side of the person lying down. He places his left hand on the forehead and his right hand on the solar plexus. The third masseur is also on the right side. His right hand lies on the left hipbone and his left hand on the right shoulder. The fourth is on the left side and places his right hand on the left shoulder and his left on the hipbone. The fifth is on the right side of the recumbent person. His right hand clasps the left foot and his left hand clasps the right hand of the person being treated. The sixth is on the left side. His left hand clasps the right foot and with his right hand he holds the left hand of the person.

All begin to chant the mantram 'OM.' The masseurs in positions three and four rhythmically swing the pelvis of the person lying down. After five or ten minutes they all stop chanting. Their hands remain a little longer on the places indicated and they feel the energy. Then, they raise their hands about a foot above their position and finally remove them after one or two minutes. The one who has received the massage rests as long as he likes. After his rest, he may, if he wishes give an account of what he has experienced.

The Great Circle

In order to form this great circle, a group of eight is necessary. They lie down side by side in a circle with their feet pointing towards the centre. Their hands complete the circuit by touching each other lightly with the tips of their fingers. Their legs are spread out, the right foot being in contact with the left foot of the partner on the right. Energy is received with the left hand and the left foot and passed on with the right hand and the right foot.

Each member of the group concentrates on passing on 'love.' It is also possible to pass on:

OM	light
healing	endlessness
peace	now
bliss	perfection
light	

5. Meditation

Every meditation technique provides a possibility of overcoming the polarities in oneself.

Mediation techniques may be classified according to their points of departure as follows: body meditations, spirit meditations, nature meditations. I will give a few possible examples. All meditations have the aim of purifying the consciousness in order to recognise and experience ever greater perfection.

Sit relaxed with your back straight and your eyes closed. Do not expect anything. Observe and accept what happens. This inward and outward attitude is the basis of almost every meditation and is meditation itself.

Yin-Yang

Empty yourself and let the yin-yang symbol appear before your inward eye. Let it have its effect on you.

Energy-breathing

Inhale into your pelvis. Breathe out from your pelvis to the centre of your head. Breathe in from your head back to your pelvis. Breathe out from your pelvis to your head.

Energy-breathing-heart

Spread your arms out gently sideways. Breathe in through your mouth. Observe the movement of breath in your chest. Consciously let the stream of breath go to your heart. As you breathe out love will shine out of your heart.

Abdomen-breathing-energy

Breathe towards a point just under your navel (vitality chakra). Breathe from this point through your abdomen out into the world.

The Four Elements

Relax. Shut your eyes. Let the earth energy come into you. Observe. Let earth energy be replaced by water energy. Be entirely water energy. Fire replaces water. Let fire energy rise up in you. Be entirely fire energy. Let air energy come. It replaces fire energy. Be entirely air energy. *Be all four elements.*

Meditation Exercises: to balance the energies of the body within a short time. On the outbreath try to relax more deeply each time. Imagine how, while breathing out, you are extending the force field of your body more and more outwards, until it is about nine to twelve feet thick all round your body. Relax. Let floods of water flow through you from head to foot. Let the waves get smaller and smaller until the surface of the water is smooth like the sea on a calm day.

Colours

Visualise a colour. This colour runs through your feet up to the crown of your head and fills you up completely. Then, let it flow back into the earth through your feet. Begin with black, then go over to grey, then take in turn light brown, dark brown, dark red, orange, yellow, green, pink, blue, violet, gold, silver, white. It is not necessary to go through all the colours every time. Your situation probably only calls for certain colour changes in order to balance your energy. You can proceed as follows: sit calmly and relaxedly and enquire inwardly which colour switch you can profitably use in your present situation. Then, let that colour come and do the exercise with it. This colour (there may be several, one after the other) controls the domestic economy of your energy.

Body meditation

Sit down and direct your attention towards your body. Observe and accept.

Energy balance by means of Polarity Word Meditation

As already described, energy blocks in the body may also be regarded as providing information and impulse. If the information contained in the retained energy is addressed direct, a reaction will follow. This should be carried out as follows: let the word 'contentment' appear before your inward eye. Look at it. Observe how it emerges before your inward eye. Let it have its effect on you.

Observe your body. What happens to it? Are you experiencing greater contentment or does some other feeling arise? Let the effect continue. Observe your body's reactions. Remain uninvolved, a neutral observer. Accept all reactions. By using this word in this meditative form you will be addressing the polarity contentment/discontentment. The word 'contentment' appearing before your inward eye acts as polarity to the corresponding information contained in the energy blocks in the body. The polarisation of work and body energies activates forces which finally lead to harmony.

If you are balanced as far as 'contentment' is concerned, that is to say, if there is no longer any invasion of energy in the word, then you will no longer have any reaction in your body. You will know what this word means for you, experience it and actually be it. We all have the experience of reacting strongly to certain words. Some words are trigger words. The word 'football' makes some people's hearts beat faster. The word 'love' may produce sadness. The word 'peace' makes some people sceptical. The word 'car' produces unrest. These are examples of the correspondence between word and bodily reaction which may be observed everywhere in daily life, at home at work, etc. Reactions such as those described above show that there is a lack of balance, an invasion of energy, a block. When observing the reactions of one's body there should be no identification with the energy information. The observer

82

must release himself from the information existing inside him and at the same time accept it. This non-identification process does not need to be expressed in words. What is important is that the energy information does not make you exclaim 'That's me!'

The energy is not retained, but expends itself in a certain procedure by means of various body reactions. For example, take the word 'hate.' The word is visualized. Body reactions may be: slight unrest; increased flow of saliva; damp hands; tension throughout the body; the feeling 'I won't' arises; increased dampness of the right hand, the left hand normal again; a feeling in the right half of the body of wanting to hit out; distress in the region of the heart; again the feeling of 'I won't'; slight pain in the shoulders; tension in the jaw muscles; tightening in the upper part of the chest; a feeling that energy is flowing down from the shoulders through the arms; no further reaction when the word is visualised. In relation to the energy of hate, the subject has become calm and quiet. He is no longer bound by hate, but has observed it and accepted it. Through this procedure, the solid energy which corresponded to the hate was expended and is no longer able to influence that person in his experience, thought and action.

Word meditation may take about fifteen minutes. Afterwards, the meditator feels freer and more relaxed. He has become calmer and more active.

There are two ways of finding out by experience which is the right word meditation for you. (a) Relax and let the word you are to work with at the moment rise up inside you. Visualise it as described above. (b) Ask a friend to concentrate on you and to let a word, a sentence or a description come to him or her, with which you can then work. This also works well for polarity groups. It is also possible for the leader of the whole group to give a word with which each individual proceeds as described above.

6. Skin Stimulation

Electrical Charges

Horizontal Charges

The body may be divided horizontally into zones, bearing different charges. The feet, the pelvis, including the genitals, the lower half of the forearm, the upper part of the shoulder and the chin are negatively charged. The skin from the knee to the ankle, the upper region of the abdomen to the ribs, the upper half of the forearm, the nose, the upper jaw and the ears are neutral. The thigh, the hands, the upper arms, the chest up to the shoulder joint and the eyes, forehead and crown of the head are all positively charged.

Vertical Lines

The body may also be divided vertically. The so-called central line runs from the highest point of the crown of the head straight down to the genitals, so imaginary lines may be drawn downwards through the whole of the body.

The two divisions, horizontal and vertical, together form a system of co-ordinates enabling definite points to be found.

If you go over your skin with your finger, you will find that within an area of just an inch or two you can experience various sensations arise because the energy in or on the skin has not been equalised. Let us suppose that one such zone is in the middle of the right thigh and is therefore in a positively charged region. Now, let us visualise the vertical line and carry it over the body through all positively charged parts. If there is numbness in the skin of the thigh, then this will also be found in the other positively charged regions on the imaginary line. In addition, a corresponding numbness will probably be found in the left half of the body on the vertical line in the positive region.

Exercise: Go over your partner's skin with your finger, looking for definite sensations. Let your partner tell you about his sensations. Then look for the corresponding skin sensations in the other parts of the body by means of the division of zones. Note exactly where these skin sensations occur and let the correct polarity contacts come to you for equalising these energies. It is better to work with the fingers rather than with the whole hand. (For your guidance, remember the thumb is neutral, the index finger is negatively charged, the middle finger is positively charged, the third finger is negatively charged, the little finger is positively charged). After polarisation, test to see whether the skin in the polarised region still shows the same sensations as before. It is quite possible that only the bottom and the top stimulation points will need to be polarised in order to remove all corresponding stimulation. It is also possible that several sessions may be needed in order to achieve complete harmony.

Let yourself be guided in your work by the wisdom of the free-flowing energy, and then nothing, however seemingly unusual and inexplicable to you, will prevent the harmonising of the unequalised fields of energy. A whole book could be written about the variety of polarity contacts arising from work on skin sensations alone. Experiment with the system of coordinates described above and allow yourself to be guided.

Spots

If we consider someone with respect to his energy structure, we do not only look at the flow of energy in his body but we also see with the inward eye whether any little shining grey or black spots, about as big as a cent or a penny, can be found on his skin.

Exercise: Learn to recognise black or dark spots on your partner. If you look directly at his skin you may recognise dark circles. If you look at the region above the skin you may observe dark rays. The back is particularly suitable for this exercise. Press the dark spot with your fingers. Let yourself be guided about which finger to use, and in what order to press the spots. Perhaps the energy will guide you to press two spots at once. When you press, your partner will feel first pain at this spot and then relief. The captive energy in this spot will be released by the pressure. With your inner eye you will be able to see how the energy spreads out within your partner and gives him a greater feeling of well-being and harmony.

It is very useful to polarise the black spots with each other. For this, use the index finger and sometimes the middle finger as well. The lower spot is usually touched with the middle finger of the right hand and the spot nearer the head with the index finger of the left. If both spots are at the same level, fingers with equal charges will be used.

Energies

The dark energy imprisoned in the body was formerly free-flowing vital energy. This once-living free energy was at some time blocked up by some frightening, troublesome or frustrating experiences and this process may still be going on. Since this person was not able or willing to come to terms with what has happened, the experience became frozen and sometimes also forgotten, but the imprisoned energy bears the imprint of the experience.

The dark energy blocks distort and prevent the flow of vital energy, and in so doing forces feeling, experience, action and thought into a definite pattern. As a result of this a great deal of energy is directed towards certain habits, while advantage cannot be taken of other possibilities as long as the blocks remain. A person thinks that this unconscious choice is his individual character, 'the way he is', his fate, and because he does not have information about the true relationship between things, he mistakes this view which he has of the world for reality. That is not to say that the feelings and sensations are not real, but they are purely subjective and will remain so unless they are carried along by the flow of free, living, vital energy. A person has, at all times, a share in this energy, but it is neither rational nor emotional, but neutral and yet warm and kindly, always 'bound' to serve life, to serve the present. Imprisoned energy is not at the disposal of the here and now. It is directed towards the past or the future. Hopes, fears and uncertainties are tangible products of imprisoned energy.

Energy blocks have their inbuilt information structures which manifest in prejudices, in philosophies, in sentences beginning 'You must not, you ought not, you may not' etc. Such information is a summary of the situations in which the block arose. It is, even if unconsciously, active in people and expresses itself in the form of precepts, such as 'Be unhappy if...', 'You will get through life better if you are ill'. 'Beware of women/men, they will only make you unhappy'. Many people apparently depend on truisms such as these, thinking them the key to good fortune. If an energy block is dispersed, and with it the command or the information, then a person will direct himself more towards the here and now. He will be more objective. He no longer has the tendency and the inner compulsion to be unhappy if ... or the idea that he will get on better in life if he is ill, etc. During the course of the polarity work, he will become freer from compelling ideas about life and philosophies. He will live life as it is. He will be responsible, because he knows the right answer to everything. This answer is – Love.

A man lives through five different kinds of energy:

1. Free-flowing vital energy. This bestows life.

2. The destroying force. This destroys, breaks up, blocks everything which is in movement.

3. Negative force.

4. Positive force. These two forces are mutually limiting. Through their interchange arises the free-flowing vital energy.

5. The force for which I can find no suitable name. Words such as nothing or the absolute only hint at it. It is the inexpressible.

7. Effectiveness and Reality

Once more: What is Polarity?

Polarities are created by the limited view of human reason and, therefore, mean a limitation of life. Polarities do not really exist. They are deceptive, imaginary pictures of reality. Reality is unity, a steady stream. It is only in the present that there is no restriction. The present is a stream, comparable to the stream of vital energy between the hands. Polarities are a means to an ever deeper experience of reality. Everyone who wishes to develop further must accept polarities; but he must not identify with them, but must rather allow them to operate *in order that they may be transcended*. The polarity system is consistent in itself, but always it reflects only a partial reality from its own restricted point of view.

Yet again: What is Polarity?

Polarity work uses polarities in order to overcome them in the end.
Polarity is a *method*.
Polarity sees a person as a whole.
Polarity offers a person as the possibility of evolving completely.

For whom is Polarity suitable?

Polarity is suitable for people who wish to escape from an unsatisfactory situation into greater harmony.

Polarity helps people to expand in certain spheres, giving them:
greater vitality
greater learning ability
greater harmony of movement
better concentration
more calm
more creativity
more enjoyment of life
more and more the sense of being present in oneself.

Polarity helps people who wish to free themselves from:
unrest
stress
discontentment
dullness
egoism
unkindness
unconsciousness and fears

Who can use Polarity?

Everyone – in every person there exists polarities between which the life force flows. Everyone could learn the technique of polarity balancing in order to use them in the family, at school, in the kindergarten, in shops, in sports centres, in self-experience and development groups.

Examples of Actual Cases

Example 1: 'P.', a young man of 25 with a strong religious commitment, comes to polarity sessions because he must become 'clean'. He has to go to church regularly; he has to get up very early in the morning; he must always remember to be religious.

Distribution of energy: His crown chakra is slightly open, likewise his spleen chakra. All other chakras are closed. There is hardly any life energy in his arms and legs. The flow of energy in his spine is very weak. Consciousness of his body is very slightly developed. He does not consciously reject sexuality, but his experience of it is practically non-existent.

In the course of twelve polarity sessions stretching over a period of twenty-four weeks he slowly comes back to earth. At first he is given the task of doing the root exercise regularly once a day – with no very great success. Only very small roots form on his feet. Through polarity word meditation he learns to pay more and more attention to his body and to listen to its signals. He observes himself and discovers that he is entitled to sexuality after all. The more deeply he experiences his sexuality, the more he becomes freed from his compulsions. Vital energy is able to flow better and better in him. The ice in his pelvis is melted away. The lead weight in his chest dissolves. He becomes on considerably better terms with himself and his body and obviously feels much better.

Example 2: 'Mrs. J.' a 40 year-old housewife, has experienced misunderstandings of every kind with her husband, ever since they were first married nineteen years ago. Being very conservative, she has not found it possible to arrange her marriage satisfactorily, or to have it dissolved.

Distribution of energy: Her vital energy has been lost, except for a minimal amount in her pelvis.

She applies herself very well to polarity balancing. Almost every time she uses polarity word meditation this leads to violent reactions in the retained energy which is causing the block. Each time she feels great relief, but at first the energy is not fully liberated.

During the course of the sessions, the vital energy in her back becomes completely stabilised, so that the forehead chakra can be cleared. The energy which has become stuck there is discharged within a few seconds. The thoughts about her misery and her marriage which kept going round and round in her head evaporate. Her head has cleared. She says that the whole burden of nineteen years of unhappy marriage has been removed by these polarity sessions. After fourteen meetings, she has gained enough strength and objectivity to be responsible for the fate of her marriage.

Example 3: 'Ch.' a 42 year-old commercial artist comes to polarity sessions. He has described himself as very restless, easily provoked, basically discontented without any tangible cause. He is becoming less and less interested in his work, which he used to find very satisfying.

Distribution of energy: His body and his head are isolated. There is scarcely any energy left in his arms. He has a great deal of blocked energy round his head, chest and abdomen.

After seventeen meetings of polarity work, his discontentment, his restlessness and the bad effect on his work have disappeared. The solid energy in abdomen and chest has partly discharged into the earth and partly been used for the benefit of his work. After the overloading had been adjusted, the vital energy had no difficulty in connecting head and body. Then the circling energy stuck round the head could also be discharged. During the final polarity sessions, he learned a meditation technique which is helping his further development.

Example 4: 'K.' a 26 year-old housewife, the mother of two children, wishes to have eight polarity sessions in order to make inward progress. After these sessions, she has become considerably more alert, active and calm. Now that she has a wider perspective, greater endurance and more manual dexterity. She takes less time over her daily chores in the house and can devote herself more to herself and her children. The time saved she also uses to further her education. She has heightened consciousness of her body. Small ailments have disappeared. She is in a position to put right her own body energy, which sometimes gets out of order. In these eight sessions, the work has all been with polarity contacts, which have made the energy flow over whole sections of her body.

Example 5: A 40 year-old teacher also comes, so he says, in order to develop further. He says he has no explicit difficulties.

Distribution of energy: Little energy in the spine. Excessive energy stagnation in the head and dark, cloudy energy all round the body. He does not apply himself to word meditation. Polarity contacts caused very little movement of energy in him. His body was governed by a completely overpowering 'no', with which he identified entirely. He did not want to give up this identification because he did not want to have anything to do with his body. After the fourth meeting we parted.

Example 6: A young man in his middle twenties arrives unexpectedly, talking in a confused way with jerky movements. He immediately tells me that he has no work and no friends.

On being given a complete earthing exercise with intake of energy through the feet, he feels energy coming into his whole body through the feet and legs. While doing so, he has to breathe very deeply and intensively. After this exercise he goes away calmly and quietly. He is advised to do the earthing exercise several times a week.

Example 7: 'D' is a 23 year-old male, who comes to polarity sessions in order to increase the flow of his body energy. For four years he has taken part in Far-eastern martial arts and this has given him much pleasure and success. He describes himself as a person who is active, but who has for some time been feeling that he is not getting on as he should.

Distribution of energy: His feet are separated from his body at the ankles. He carries a load of solid energy around with him inside and on his back. The energy of his head is cut off from that of the body. His arms at the shoulders are connected with his chest by only a little energy. I talk over his energy distribution with him. While we are speaking, part of the solid energy in his back flows down. He is given the task every day for a fortnight of spreading out his arms several times a day, feeling his hands as poles and letting energy flow between these poles. At the end of the fortnight, the energy blocks in the shoulder joints have been removed. With the aid of polarity contacts, the connection between head and body is restored. At the same time, the block cutting off the feet disappears. After six sessions, he is completely calm with vitality and elasticity such as he has never known before. His movements are more fluent, more graceful and more powerful. He now has more success in his martial arts.

Basic Principles

Every person is complete, but he must first experience this completeness.

Thoughts, feelings and emotions can be mistaken – life and the vital force can never be mistaken.

Here and now is the path.
The end of the journey is the unity of here and now.

Everything is possible.

Polarities do not exist. They are the product of our reason.
What does exist is the continual flow of vital energy.

Everything comes and goes.
The all remains.

It is love which heals, not I.

Surrender to life which heals, not I.

From love comes loving.
From loving comes love.
Love is loving.

The Zero Point

A man's life usually takes its course between the following polarities:

positive	negative
joy	fear
love	hate
togetherness	loneliness
order	chaos
riches	poverty
health	sickness
beauty	ugliness
peace	stress
contentment	discontentment
life	death
construction	destruction
work	lack of work
good fortune	misfortune
elation	depression
brightness	dullness
strength	weakness

A person goes up and down between these poles. If he is in a position of 'positive' polarity, he fears the 'negative' side. If he is in a 'negative' position, he will hope for the 'positive' polarity. He is always on the way from somewhere to somewhere else, so long as he is not at zero point. It is hope and fear which direct his life. He does not direct it himself.

Exciting NEW Books available from
GATEWAY BOOKS

Where There's Love *A Community and its Guiding Impulse.* by Annie Wilson.

This is a very human story of how four families gave up successful careers and started a community in the Malvern Hills, which is now a conference/study centre. They were influenced by the 'readings' and philosophy of a spirit to found the Atlantean Society thirty years ago, to bring light and hope into a society in transition.

192pp   photos   paper   £3.35   (US $6.95)

Agartha: *A Course in Cosmic Awareness*
by Meredith L. Young

The working of the Universe, the real nature of our purpose on Earth is described from material which was channelled through the author in meditation. The source has authority and conviction and this book is widely used for group study in the USA because of its practical nature. Reprogramming the conscious mind; dynamics of creating your own reality; Earth changes and the key to Earth's survival; communing with Nature and medical clairvoyance are all in this book.

304pp   Illus.   paper   £5.95   (not avail USA)

Towards a Magical Technology
by Tom Graves

Here is a challenge to the narrow vision of contemporary science. Tom Graves is not interested in theories, but as a technologist in making things work. Much true creativity has an intuitive origin and this book examines synchronicities and magic as it operates in the creative field. This controversial book draws from dowsing to computers, from radical psychology to subatomic phyics.

96pp   Illus.   paper   £3.95   (US $6.95)

Living in Time: *A close-to-life Astrology sampler*
by Palden Jenkins

This provides a language for the understanding of the nature of Time as it unfolds in our lives, suitable for beginners, samplers, reassessors and growing souls. Lunar cycles, planetary motions, time cycles and crunch points, birth charts and change are all examined with a new eye, written in a simple style, encouraging creativity and involvement. Plenty of illustrations, diagrams and projects.

224pp   Illus.   papaer   £5.95   (US $9.95)

The New Clairvoyance
by Mario Schoenmaker

Here is a guide for the increasing number of people who are becoming sensitive and clairvoyant to understand these gifts. It gives very clear descriptions and illustrations of the aura (energy field around the body); teaching about reincarnation and karma; humans as spiritual beings; the characteristics of the aura; the overself and personal symbols; advice on spiritual readings.

256pp   8pp colour   paper   £5.95   (US $9.95)

The Kabbalah & Psychology
by Z'ev Ben Shimon Halevi

Ancient and modern meet within this book, which sees psychology as concerned primarily with the mind as it relates to the body, to the soul and to the Divine, in the Kabbalistic hierarchy of levels. The notion of reincarnation and karma, prenatal existence and memory are discussed alongside new views of contemporary life and the child's relationship to its parents. This book looks at the evolution of man as human from early Shamanistic myths through to Freud and Jung.

288pp   Illus.   paper   £6.95   (not avail USA)

GATEWAY BOOKS, Selected backlist:

Open the Window: *Practical Ideas for the Lonely and Depressed* by Joan Gibson.

Now in its second edition. This practical, caring helpful book has brought hope to thousands of lonely people.

"Only someone who has known depression could write such a warm and personal book" *Therapy Weekly.* "Easy to read, full of commonsense... a sprinkling of humour. ... Very much recommended" *Science of Thought Rev.*

128pp   paper   £3.95   (US $6.95)

Finding a Way: *A Realist's Introduction to Self-Help Therapy* by Alex Howard

"This exceptionally helpful and down-to-earth book is a revealing, teach yourself course in removing those masks we hide behind, in getting to know ourselves and others better... providing many practical guidelines of who we really are and how much we can truly give to each other. I strongly recommend this valuable book" *Science of Thought Rev.*

224pp   paper   £4.95   (US $7.95)

Choose Happiness: *and begin to take control of your life* by Elizabeth Smith

A programme of self-observation to see where we are blocking the energy of our own potential – such as by worrying about other people's expectations. Out of her own determination to start making choices, Elizabeth Smith in later life discovered the *est* and *Insight* training workshops. She has woven this material with the model of personal integration from *Gestalt* psychology, together with her own experience into a very practical and straightforward book.

192pp   paper   £3.95   (US $6.95)

Fruits of the Moon Tree: *The Medicine Wheel and Transpersonal Psychology* by Alan Bleakley

This psychological process of maturation, by which each of us must come to terms with the masculine and feminine within us, is described in this major new work. Drawing on images of Celtic lore, of classical mythology and fairy tale, archetypes and dreams, Alan Bleakley relates these to North American Indian Medicine Wheel teachings which stress the healing qualities of plants, animals, the earth – Nature herself.

320pp   120 illus.   paper   £6.95   (US $10.95)

The Passionate Life: *Stages of Loving* by Sam Keen

Sexuality as a vehicle for creative growth is just one of the themes in this "Treasury of wisdom and insight" George Leonard (au. of *The End of Sex*). Keen describes the natural expression of sexuality at each stage of life but also the perversion ususally found in our emotionally impoverished society. "In a free-wheeling colloquial style this wise and beautiful essay breathes new life into our thinking about love and sexuality" *Publishers Weekly.*

288pp   illus.   £4.95   (not avail. USA)

Something is Happening: *Spiritual Awareness and Depth Psychology* by Winifred Rushforth

A book of profound wisdom that has already achieved the status of a classic, it shows how the spiritual and psychological ways of understanding are one; both bound up with the healing process that must take place before we can become mature and whole human beings. Winifred Rushforth pioneered therapeutic and creative groupwork in Scotland where she was well known for her religious broadcasts.

160pp   paper   £3.95   (US $6.95)

Please write to us if you wish for a complete catalogue:
GATEWAY BOOKS, 19 Circus Place, Bath, BA1 2PW
USA: INTERBROOK Inc, 14895 14th St. San Leandro, CA 94577